A Son's Quest for Healing after Dad's Passing: A Journey of Reflection, Resilience, and Self-Discovery

I0842499

Robert P. Stringer

About the Author

Robert P. Stringer is a dedicated historian with a deep passion for uncovering the stories of the past. His love for history is matched by his interest in travel, which allows him to experience firsthand the places and cultures he studies. Through his travels, Robert has developed a unique perspective on how history, culture, and personal experiences intersect.

With a Ph.D. in History, Robert has spent decades teaching, writing, and lecturing on various historical topics, making complex subjects accessible and engaging to a wide audience

In addition to his professional work, Robert is an avid reader and a documentary enthusiast. He believes in the power of storytelling to educate, inspire, and connect people across time and space. This belief is evident in his writing, where he strives to bring historical events and personal experiences to life for his readers.

Acknowledgements

Writing the book, "A Son's Quest for Healing After Dad's Passing" inspired by my own real-life experiences, has been a journey of discovery, empathy, and resilience. I am sincerely grateful to authors whose deep insights and experiences in the field of grief and healing have enriched and informed this work. Special thanks to Dr. Elisabeth Kübler-Ross, whose pioneering work on the stages of grief provided a foundation for understanding this poignant journey. I am also indebted to C.S. Lewis for his touching reflections on loss in his book "A Grief Observed," which resonated deeply with the themes explored in this book.

Heartfelt gratitude goes to my editor, Karen L. Drake, for her insightful feedback and dedication to refining this manuscript. Her expertise has been extremely useful in shaping the final narrative, ensuring that the themes of loss, healing, and resilience are conveyed with clarity and compassion.

I extend sincere thanks to my family for their unwavering love and support throughout the creation of this book. To my wife, Hope, your belief in me and your encouragement have been a constant source of strength to me. To my son, your patience and understanding during this process have meant the world to me.

Most importantly, I am profoundly grateful to my father, whose memory is the heartbeat of this book. His love, wisdom, and enduring spirit continue to illuminate my path and shape my journey. This book stands as a tribute to his life and the profound influence he has had on mine.

I am grateful to the numerous friends, colleagues, and supporters whose encouragement has motivated me to share this story with the world. Your faith in the significance of this narrative has propelled me forward.

In conclusion, I dedicate this book to the cherished memory of loved ones everywhere, whose lives have touched ours in different ways. Their presence continues to inspire us, reminding us of the enduring power of love and remembrance. May their stories live on, influencing our lives and guiding us with their wisdom and grace.

To the readers who will embark on this journey, I hope this book offers comfort, insight, and a sense of connection during your own path of healing. This book reflects not only personal experiences but also the collective strength of families navigating loss.

With heartfelt appreciation,

Robert P. Stringer

Introduction: Remembering Dad

In the quiet moments of dawn, when the world is still wrapped in the tender embrace of sleep, Mark Reynolds often finds himself drawn back to the memory of his father. His laughter, his wisdom, his unwavering presence, all of it floods Mark's mind like the first light of day. These memories have become guiding stars in a sky that once seemed endlessly dark. "A Son's Quest for Healing after Dad's Passing," is not just a book about a trip; it is an intimate disquisition of grief, resilience, and the rediscovery of self.

Mark Reynolds' story begins in a place we all hope never to visit but inevitably do—the moment of losing a loved one. For Mark, that moment came like a thief in the night, stealing away the man who had been his anchor and mentor, his father. His passing was sudden, leaving behind a void that seemed impossible to fill. Grief, Mark learned, is not a single emotion but a complex array of feelings, such as pain, confusion, anger, and, strangely, love. This book is born from that grief, showing the enduring bond between a father and his son, and the transformative power of loss.

In the days following his father's death, Mark felt adrift in a sea of emotions. The weight of his absence was crushing, and he struggled to find his footing. Every corner of their home seemed haunted by his presence. His favorite chair, the scent of his cologne lingering in the air, the sound of his voice echoing in his mind. It was in these moments of deep sorrow that Mark realized he needed to embark on a trip, not just a physical one, but an emotional and spiritual quest to heal and rediscover himself.

Setting out on this adventure was not a decision made lightly. It required leaving behind the familiar, stepping away from the life he had built, and venturing into the unknown. The first steps were the hardest, filled with doubt and fear. Mark questioned his sanity. He wondered if he was running away from his pain rather than confronting it. But deep down, he knew this journey was necessary. It was a chance to honor his father, to seek answers to the questions his death had left behind, and to find a way to move forward.

As Mark traveled from place to place, the world opened up to him in ways he had never imagined. Each city, each landscape, held its own lessons and revelations. In busy streets, he found solace in the anonymity of the crowd, a reminder that life continues even in the face of loss. In quiet places, he discovered the power of silence and reflection, learning to listen to the whispers of his soul. In the vast deserts like that of Arizona, he learnt resilience and the ability to endure and thrive even in the harshest conditions.

These travels were not just about seeing new places but about connecting with the essence of life itself. Mark met people from all walks of life, each with their own stories of loss and healing. Their courage inspired him, reminding him that he was not alone in his grief. In sharing his story with them, he found a sense of community and understanding that was completely healing. These connections, these shared moments of vulnerability, became the threads that wove his journey together.

Throughout this journey, Mark was constantly reminded of his father's wisdom. His father had always taught him the importance of finding strength in adversity. His words echoed in Mark's mind, guiding him through the darkest moments. "Life is not about avoiding the storms," he would say, "but about learning to dance in the rain." These words became Mark's mantra, a source of strength that carried him through the toughest times.

One of the most profound lessons Mark learned was the importance of embracing vulnerability. For so long, he had equated vulnerability with weakness, a sign of failure. But as he opened himself up to his pain, he realized that vulnerability is a powerful source of strength. It allows us to connect deeply with others, to find empathy and understanding, and to heal from the inside out. By embracing his own vulnerability, Mark found the courage to face his grief head-on, to let go of the need to be strong all the time, and to allow himself to heal.

This journey also led Mark to a deeper understanding of family. In reconnecting with his loved ones, he discovered the healing power of shared memories and stories. It made him remember his father in all his complexity, his strengths, his flaws, his love. These moments of connection were not just about reminiscing but about finding a way to carry his legacy forward. His father had always been the glue that held their family together, and in his absence, they learned to create new bonds to support each other in ways they had never done before.

In the process of rediscovering himself, Mark confronted many of his deepest fears and insecurities. He learned to accept himself fully, to acknowledge both his strengths and his weaknesses. This acceptance was liberating, allowing him to let go of the expectations and judgments that had weighed him down for so long. It opened up new possibilities for him, new paths for personal growth and fulfillment. Mark realized that self-discovery is not about changing who we are but about embracing our true selves, with all our imperfections and potential.

Finding closure and moving forward was perhaps the most challenging part of Mark's journey. It required a delicate balance of honoring his father's memory while letting go of the past. He came to understand that closure is not about forgetting but about integrating our losses into our lives in a way that allows us to move forward. It is about finding peace with what was and embracing what is. As Mark navigated this path, he found that his father's presence was not confined to the past but lived on in his actions, his choices, and his love.

As you embark on this journey with Mark through the pages of this book, it is hoped that you find not just a story of loss and healing but a source of inspiration and strength. Grief is a universal experience, one that touches each of us in different ways.

The hope is that by sharing Mark's journey, a glimpse of hope and strength can be offered to those who are struggling with their own losses. Healing is not a destination but a journey, one that requires patience, courage, and a willingness to embrace the unknown.

This book depicts the enduring power of love and the human spirit. It is a reminder that even in our darkest moments, there is light to be found, lessons to be learned, and strength to be gained. It is an invitation to explore the depths of our emotions, to connect with others in meaningful ways, and to find our own unique paths to healing and self-discovery.

Thank you for joining Mark on this journey. May the stories and lessons within these pages inspire you, comfort you, and remind you of the incredible resilience of the human spirit. As we walk this path together, let us carry forward the love and wisdom of those we have lost, and find the courage to embrace the future with hope and gratitude.

Chapter 1: The Call of Grief

Thinking of Dad

Grief descends like a heavy mist, enveloping the world in a haze of sorrow. For Mark Reynolds, the passing of his father, Jonathan Reynolds, shattered the familiar rhythm of life, leaving behind emptiness. Jonathan, a pillar of strength and wisdom, had guided Mark through life's ups and downs with unwavering support and love. His absence now echoed through empty rooms and silent corridors, a stark reminder of the void left behind.

In the immediate aftermath of Jonathan's unexpected departure, Mark found himself grappling with emotions that ranged from disbelief to overwhelming sadness. Grief, he realized, was not just the absence of a loved one but a complex blend of feelings ranging from anger to confusion, and a deep yearning for one last conversation. Memories flooded his mind: the sound of Jonathan's laughter echoing through family gatherings, the warmth of his reassuring embrace during difficult times. Each memory was a lifeline, anchoring Mark to a past that suddenly felt both distant and achingly present.

In the weeks following the funeral, Mark often found himself retreating to his father's favorite spot by the river, a peaceful place where they had spent countless hours fishing and talking about life. Sitting by the water, Mark could almost hear his father's voice. He always felt his presence. It was here, in the solitude of nature, that Mark began to confront the depth of his grief. He would sit for hours, letting the tears flow freely, allowing himself to feel the raw pain without trying to push it away.

Mark's nights were filled with dreams of his father. In these dreams, they would relive childhood adventures where they would build forts in the backyard, race their bikes down the old dirt road, whisper secrets under the cover of darkness. These dreams were both a comfort and a torment. He would wake up, heart heavy with the realization that his father was no longer there. Yet, they also served as a bridge, connecting him to his father in a realm where time and space seemed irrelevant.

During the day, Mark immersed himself in sorting through his father's belongings, each item a palpable connection to his father's life. The process was bittersweet. He would find old photographs tucked away in books, mementos from family vacations, and letters they had exchanged during college. One afternoon, he stumbled upon his father's journal, filled with entries that revealed his father's innermost thoughts and dreams. Reading his father's words, Mark felt a profound sense of closeness, as if he was glancing at a part of his father that had always remained hidden. The journal entries were a revelation. His father had written about his hopes for the future, his struggles, and his love for his family. He had documented moments of doubt and triumph, leaving behind a foundation of strength and hope for what lies ahead.

Mark's journey through grief was not linear; it was a winding path with moments of darkness and light. There were days when the pain felt unbearable, and others when he felt a renewed sense of hope and strength. He learned to be gentle with himself, to honor his emotions, and to seek support when needed. Through it all, the memories of his father remained a guiding light, reminding him of the love they had shared and the enduring bond that death could not sever.

In embracing his loss, Mark discovered a deeper understanding of life and the human experience. He realized that grief was proof of the depth of the love he had for his father, and that by keeping his father's memory alive, he could find a way to navigate the complexities of his own feelings. The journey was arduous, but it was also filled with moments of immense connection and insight. Mark emerged from the depths of his grief with a renewed appreciation for the fragility and beauty of life, carrying his father's spirit with him as he continued his path forward.

Facing the Unknown

As Mark explored the uncharted territory of grief, he confronted a series of questions about life and loss. How does one reconcile the permanence of death with the fleeting nature of human existence? In moments of solitude, he sought solace in cherished mementos, for example, a well-worn book from Jonathan's library, a faded photograph capturing a moment of shared joy. These tangible reminders became portals to the past, offering comfort in the midst of uncertainty.

The nights were particularly challenging for Mark. Alone in the quiet of his room, he found himself grappling with existential questions that seemed to have no easy answers. Why do we lose the ones we love? What is the purpose of our brief time on this earth? These questions haunted him, making sleep difficult to catch. During these sleepless nights, he often found himself reaching for his father's old journal. The familiar scrawl of his father's handwriting was a balm to his troubled mind, providing a sense of closeness and continuity.

As he faced the unknown, Mark began to understand that healing was not about finding definitive answers, but about learning to live with the questions. He realized that grief was a journey, not a destination, and that each step forward was an attestation to his resilience and courage. The uncertainty that once filled him with fear began to transform into a sense of possibility, as he embraced the idea that the future, while unknown, held the potential for growth and discovery.

As Mark embraced the unknown, he carried with him the lessons he had learned from his father. He understood that while the pain of loss would never completely disappear, it could coexist with the joy of living.

Seeking Solace in Memories

Amidst the turmoil of grief, Mark found solace in the ritual of remembrance. He revisited familiar places they had once frequented together, the quiet park benches where father and son had shared conversations that covered the full spectrum of life, the lively city streets where Jonathan's presence had infused every corner with warmth and laughter. Each visit was a pilgrimage emphasizing the enduring bond they had shared and the legacy Jonathan had left behind.

Mark would often sit on their favorite bench in the park, under the canopy of an ancient oak tree, where the rustling leaves whispered tales of their past. He remembered how

Jonathan would listen intently, offering advice with the wisdom that only a father could impart. These memories, though heartbreaking, became a source of strength for Mark. It brought to mind the values his father had instilled in him, particularly kindness, perseverance, and bravery in facing life's challenges.

In the crowded streets of the city, Mark found himself drawn to a small, cozy café where they had spent countless hours. The aroma of freshly brewed coffee and the hum of conversation brought back vivid memories of Jonathan's infectious laughter and his knack for making even mundane moments special. Mark would sit at their usual table, sipping his coffee slowly, and allow the memories to wash over him. Each visit to the café was like a warm embrace, a way to feel connected to his father despite the physical absence.

He also revisited the seaside town where they had taken family vacations. Walking along the sandy shores, Mark would always imagine hearing Jonathan's voice calling out to him, encouraging him to explore and discover the wonders of the world. The rhythmic sound of the waves crashing against the shore became a soothing backdrop as Mark reflected on the lessons his father had taught him about embracing change and finding beauty in the everyday.

These journeys were more than just visits to places; they were journeys into the heart of his relationship with his father. The memories were not just relics of the past but living parts of Mark's present, guiding him as he navigated his path forward.

Chapter 2: Setting Out on a Journey

Deciding to Depart

Mark Reynolds stood at a crossroads of emotions after the unexpected passing of his father. In the quiet moments that followed, amidst the echoes of shared memories and the weight of grief, Mark made a pivotal decision. He resolved to embark on a journey that would take him far from the usual comforts of home. It wasn't simply an escape; it was a deliberate choice to confront his emotions, explore the world as his father once did, and seek solace in the vastness of new horizons.

Jonathan had always instilled in Mark a love for adventure. From childhood road trips across the American heartland to summers spent hiking in national parks, the elder Reynolds had passed down not just a sense of wanderlust but a deeper appreciation for the beauty and diversity of the world. Now, faced with the void left by his father's absence, Mark felt drawn to continue this legacy of exploration, a journey not just of miles but of rebirth and self-discovery.

Leaving Familiar Grounds

The day of departure arrived, filled with anticipation, apprehension, and a quiet determination to honor his father's memory through exploration. Mark carefully packed his essentials. Each item he took was a connection to his past and a guiding light for the journey ahead. Stepping out into the crisp morning air, he felt a blend of wistfulness and resolve, ready to embrace whatever lay beyond the horizon.

The airport was a hive of activity, a symphony of languages and cultures converging in a shared space of departure and arrival. As Mark checked in his luggage and passed through security, he couldn't help but reflect on the impermanence of life, the fleeting moments that bound people together, even in the face of loss. It was a humbling reminder of the interconnectedness of human experience, a theme that would echo throughout his voyage.

The Road Ahead

Mark's journey took him across diverse landscapes, each with its own rhythm and story to tell. From the busy streets of urban metropolises where skyscrapers kissed the sky to the serene tranquility of rural countryside painted in hues of green and gold, every mile traversed was a step closer to understanding both the world and himself.

As Mark navigated through cities teeming with life, he marveled at the intricate dance of humanity, each person playing a vital role in the complex fabric of existence. The cacophony of voices, the rush of daily life, and the constant motion mirrored the internal journey he was on. In these moments, he realized that the heartbeat of a city was not just in its physical architecture but in the collective aspirations, struggles, and dreams of its inhabitants.

Contrastingly, the vast expanses of open fields and quiet villages offered a different kind of contemplation. Here, time seemed to slow, allowing Mark to breathe deeply and contemplate the simplicity of life. The gentle rustling of leaves, the distant call of birds, and the soft whisper of the wind became his companions, offering comfort and understanding. In these serene settings, he found space to reflect on his past, confront his fears, and embrace the person he was becoming.

The journey also presented countless opportunities for growth and learning. Mark encountered challenges that tested his endurance, pushing him to dig deeper and find the strength he didn't know he possessed. There were moments of doubt and fatigue, but with each obstacle overcome, he felt a renewed sense of resolve and commitment. The road ahead was not always smooth, but it was in the rough patches that he discovered the true essence of perseverance and the beauty of the human spirit.

Every interaction along the way added layers to his understanding of life's complexities. Conversations with strangers turned into meaningful exchanges with each story shared illuminating new facets of love, loss, hope, and redemption. Mark began to see that despite the differences in culture, language, and background, there was a universal thread of humanity that connected everyone. This realization brought a sense of unity and empathy, enriching his journey with deeper meaning.

As he continued to move forward, the landscapes became more than just backdrops to his travels. They were indeed integral to his story. The vibrant colors of the world, the diverse sounds, and the myriad of scents all contributed to the richness of his experiences. Mark learned to appreciate the present moment, finding joy in the simple act of being, and discovering beauty in the mundane.

The road ahead stretched infinitely, filled with promise and uncertainty. Mark knew that his journey was just beginning and there were still many paths to explore, lessons to learn, and memories to create. With a heart full of gratitude and an open mind, he embraced the unknown, ready to face whatever awaited him. He understood that the destination was not the goal, but the journey itself was what mattered. The road ahead was a symbol of life's infinite possibilities, and Mark was ready to embrace it with an open heart and a spirit of adventure, knowing that the best was yet to come.

Lessons from the Road

As Mark traversed ancient cobblestone streets and modern highways alike, he unearthed hidden treasures of wisdom embedded in history. Conversations with locals, whose lives intertwined with the land they called home, revealed timeless truths about community, and the enduring power of human connection in the face of adversity.

In a quaint village nestled amidst the rolling hills of the Italian countryside, Mark encountered an elderly man named Giovanni, whose life revolved around nurturing his vineyard. The air was infused with the scent of ripe grapes and the earthy aroma of freshly tilled soil, inviting Mark into a world where time seemed to slow to the rhythm of seasons.

Giovanni welcomed Mark with open arms and a warm smile, inviting him to share a meal of homemade pasta and robust local wine under the shade of an ancient olive tree. As they savored each bite, Giovanni spoke passionately about the art of winemaking, a tradition passed down through generations in his family. He recounted stories of adaptation and of how each year's harvest reflected the bounty of the land and the dedication of those who tended it.

With animated gestures, Giovanni described the delicate balance of nurturing vines from tender shoots in spring to the meticulous pruning and patiently waiting for the grapes to ripen in the summer sun. He spoke of the challenges of unpredictable weather and the triumphs of a successful harvest, likening it to life's journey which has always been full of highs and lows, growth and setbacks, yet ultimately rewarding for those who persisted with patience and steadfastness.

Mark listened intently, captivated by Giovanni's wisdom and the timeless truths in his stories. As the sun dipped below the horizon, casting a golden glow over the vineyard, Giovanni shared anecdotes of love and loss, of dreams fulfilled and dreams deferred. He spoke of his late wife Maria, whose laughter once echoed through their home located in the hills, and how her spirit continued to inspire him to embrace life's changes with grace.

In that tranquil setting, surrounded by the legacy of generations past and the promise of seasons to come, Mark found comfort and deep insights into his own journey. He realized that endurance wasn't just about weathering storms but also about embracing the fluctuations of life's currents with an open heart and a steadfast spirit.

As Mark bid farewell to Giovanni and the village that had welcomed him as family, he carried with him a renewed perspective, one that celebrated the interdependence of all life and the beauty found in every stage of growth and transformation. Giovanni's lessons had become a guiding light, illuminating Mark's path forward with a deeper appreciation for the enduring power of human connection and the wisdom found in embracing life's inevitable changes.

Embracing Solitude

One of the most profound lessons Mark learned was the value of solitude. In the quiet moments between destinations, when the buzz of city life faded into the background and nature enveloped him in its embrace, he found a sense of peace that had eluded him in the busy streets and crowded airports. Whether hiking through mist covered mountains or strolling along deserted beaches at sunset, these moments of solitude became a sanctuary where he could reflect, recharge, and reconnect with himself.

In the remote wilderness of Patagonia, where jagged peaks pierced the sky and glacial lakes shimmered under the Southern Cross, Mark found himself immersed in a solitude that was both liberating and enlightening.

Patagonia's vast landscapes offered Mark a canvas of solitude unlike any he had ever experienced. Trekking through rugged trails that wound through ancient forests and beside roaring rivers, he discovered a quietude that spoke volumes. Each step carried him deeper into the heart of nature's grandeur, away from the noise of civilization and into a different realm.

One memorable evening, as he camped beside a pristine lake framed by snow-capped mountains, Mark witnessed a sunset that painted the sky in hues of pink and gold. Sitting on a boulder, with only the sound of wind rustling through the trees and water gently lapping at the shore, he felt a serene sense of peace wash over him. Here, in the embrace of solitude, Mark found understanding amidst the twists of his journey.

In moments like these, solitude became more than just being alone. It became a refuge for introspection and self-discovery. Away from the distractions of everyday life, Mark found himself reflecting on the experiences that had shaped him, contemplating his aspirations and fears, and finding solace in the vastness of nature's beauty.

During long hikes through Patagonia's untamed wilderness, Mark encountered wildlife that seemed undisturbed by his presence. He saw a condor soaring overhead and a guanaco grazing peacefully in the distance. These encounters reminded him of the connection all living things had and reinforced his appreciation for the quiet moments that allowed him to observe and connect with the natural world.

As night fell over the rugged terrain, Mark would sit by a crackling campfire, its warm glow illuminating the shadows cast by towering cliffs. Under a canopy of stars that seemed to stretch infinitely across the sky, he contemplated the mysteries of the universe and his place within it, giving him a renewed sense of direction.

Patagonia's solitude taught Mark that being alone did not equate to loneliness but rather, it offered an opportunity to reconnect with himself and his surroundings. It was a time to listen to the whispers of his heart, to nurture his inner strength, and to appreciate the beauty of simplicity in a world often defined by chaos and intricacy.

In the end, Mark's journey through Patagonia's solitude became a transformative experience for him, giving him the zeal to embrace moments of quiet reflection and finding peace amidst the raw beauty of nature. He discovered the wisdom that solitude brings which is the ability to find serenity within oneself and to embrace life's journey with a renewed sense of purpose.

Chapter 3: Reflections Along the Way

Moments of Clarity

As Mark Reynolds continued his journey, each new destination offered moments of profound clarity that shaped his understanding of both the world and himself. In the ancient city of Rome, amidst the grandeur of the Colosseum and the elements of history surrounding its ruins, Mark found himself contemplating the fleeting nature of human existence. Standing under the arches gladiators once fought for glory, he realized how small yet significant his own life was in the vast space of time.

The sun was setting, casting a warm golden shadow over the timeworn stones. Mark could almost hear the distant roars of the crowd. He could feel the anticipation that must have hung in the air. It was a place where life and death had played out in stark, brutal clarity, a reminder of the impermanence and fragility of human life. Yet, amid this harsh reality, there was a strange sense of peace. The Colosseum, despite its bloody history, testifies to the enduring spirit of humanity.

Walking through the cobbled streets of Rome, Mark was struck by the juxtaposition of ancient ruins and modern life. The city was alive with the hustle and bustle of everyday existence. Vendors were seen selling their wares, children playing in the piazzas, while tourists marveled at the historical sites. It was a city that had seen empires rise and fall, yet it continued to thrive.

In one of these moments, Mark found himself standing before the Pantheon. Its imposing columns and grand dome were marvels of engineering and architecture. Inside, the light streamed through the oculus, creating a celestial spotlight that seemed to connect the heavens to the earth. It was here, in this place of worship and contemplation, that Mark felt a sort of connection to something greater than himself. The Pantheon, with its blend of art, science, and spirituality, symbolized the interrelation of all things. Mark realized that his journey was not just about physical travel but also about exploring the depths of his own soul.

One evening, Mark ventured to the Trevi Fountain. The sound of rushing water filled the air, and the fountain's intricate sculptures glowed under the moonlight. Tradition held that throwing a coin into the fountain ensured a return to Rome. As Mark tossed his coin, he made a silent wish, not just for a return to the city, but for a return to a state of inner peace. The act, simple yet symbolic, was a reminder that wisdom often comes from letting go and trusting in the journey.

During his stay, Mark visited the Vatican City, the spiritual and administrative heart of the Roman Catholic Church. Standing in St. Peter's Basilica, surrounded by masterpieces of Renaissance art and architecture, he was overwhelmed by the sense of history and devotion that permeated the air. He spent hours gazing at Michelangelo's Pieta, absorbing the profound sorrow and beauty captured in the marble. The sculpture, with its depiction of Mary holding the body of Christ, resonated deeply with Mark, evoking his own feelings of loss and the yearning for solace.

Mark also took time to explore the quieter, lesser-known corners of Rome. He wandered through the serene gardens of Villa Borghese, finding comfort in the lush greenery and tranquil atmosphere. Here, away from the crowds and the noise, he could hear his own thoughts more clearly. Sitting on a bench, watching the swans glide across a pond, he reflected on the lessons of his journey. Clarity, he realized, often came in these moments of stillness, when the mind was free from distractions.

One particularly touching experience occurred during a visit to the Capuchin Crypt, a series of chapels decorated with the bones of thousands of Capuchin friars. The macabre yet artistic displays served as a stark reminder of mortality. A plaque in the crypt read, "What you are now, we once were; what we are now, you shall be." This message struck a chord with Mark. It was a reminder that life is transient, and that each moment should be cherished. The crypt, with its eerie beauty, offered a moment of clarity about the importance of living fully and meaningfully.

Mark's exploration of Rome wasn't just confined to its historical and spiritual landmarks. He immersed himself in the daily life of the city, savoring the simple pleasures that it had to offer. He enjoyed leisurely meals at local trattorias, where the food was a celebration of tradition and family. Sharing a meal with strangers, who quickly became friends, Mark experienced the warmth and hospitality that defined Roman culture. It was in these moments , over plates of pasta and glasses of wine, that he realized the importance of friendship and shared experiences.

Another significant moment of clarity came during a visit to the Roman Forum, the heart of ancient Rome. As Mark walked among the ruins of temples, basilicas, and government buildings, he imagined the vibrant life that once filled these spaces. The Forum, now a shadow of its former glory, was a pitiful reminder of the instability of power and the passage of time. Yet, it also symbolized firmness and renewal, as new generations built upon the foundations of the old. This lesson had a lot of meaning to Mark, reinforcing his belief in the enduring spirit of humanity.

As Mark continued to explore Rome, he encountered countless revelations that enriched his journey. Whether it was a quiet moment of reflection in a hidden courtyard, a heartfelt conversation with a local artisan, or a solitary walk along the Tiber River, each experience added a new layer of understanding. These moments were like pieces of a mosaic, coming together to form a clearer picture of his own life and the path ahead.

Through these reflections, Mark came to understand that clarity was not a destination but a continuous process of learning and growth. It was about being open to new experiences, embracing the unknown, and finding beauty in the journey itself. With each step, Mark carried these insights with him, knowing that the journey was far from over and that the lessons he had learned would continue to shape his future.

The moments of clarity he encountered along the way became the foundation upon which he built his path toward his healing and rediscovery. They illuminated the way forward, guiding him toward a deeper appreciation of life, love, and the enduring legacy of his father.

In Paris, he marveled at the grandeur of the Eiffel Tower. Standing beneath its iron lattice, Mark contemplated the layers of history and innovation that had shaped the city, a fitting metaphor for his own journey of introspection and growth.

The Eiffel Tower, with its intricate design and towering presence, stood as a symbol of durability, power and vision. As Mark gazed up at the iconic structure, he couldn't help but draw parallels between its creation and his own life's journey. Just as the tower had faced challenges during its construction, overcoming various skepticism and technical obstacles, Mark had encountered his own trials and tribulations. The tower's eventual completion and enduring legacy was proof that perseverance and determination could lead to remarkable achievements.

Strolling through the nearby Champ de Mars, Mark took in the beauty of the surrounding gardens, the laughter of children playing, and the joy of couples sharing quiet moments together. These scenes of everyday life, set against the backdrop of one of the world's most famous landmarks, reinforced the idea that even amidst grandeur, it was the simple, human experiences that truly mattered. He found solace in the thought that, like the tower, his own life was built on a foundation of both monumental moments and everyday experiences.

As he explored further, Mark visited the Musée d'Orsay, where he was captivated by the works of great artists like Monet, Van Gogh, and Degas. Each painting told a story, capturing moments of beauty, struggle, and triumph. The artists' ability to convey profound emotions through their work struck a chord with Mark. He realized that his journey, too, was a canvas with each experience a brushstroke contributing to the larger picture of his life. The museum visit became a moment of clarity, highlighting the importance of embracing both the light and shadow in his own story.

One evening, Mark found himself at a small café in Montmartre, the historic district known for its bohemian spirit and artistic heritage. As he sipped his coffee and watched the world go by, he struck up a conversation with a local artist named Camille. She spoke passionately about the importance of following one's dreams and the courage it took to live authentically. Her words echoed in Mark's mind long after their conversation ended, reminding him that his journey was not just about healing from loss, but also about honoring his true self.

The vibrant streets of Paris, with their rich history and culture, became a backdrop for Mark's self analysis. Wandering along the Seine River, he reflected on the rhythm of his own life. The river, a constant yet ever-changing presence, symbolized the journey of self-discovery. Mark found comfort in the realization that, like the river, he could navigate life's currents, embracing change and finding beauty in the journey.

The culmination of his Parisian experience came during a nighttime visit to the Eiffel Tower, where he immersed himself in its rich history and intricate details. As the tower lit up against the dark sky, Mark felt a surge of inspiration. Although Mark visited the tower during the day, nothing compared to the enchanting experience he had there at night. The illuminated structure, standing tall and proud, embodied the endurance and vitality of the human soul. As he strolled through the Gardens surrounding the tower, he marveled at the serene views it offered, feeling a sense of peace amidst the beautiful city.

His attention was captivated by the 1899 lift machinery, a marvel of engineering still in use after over a century, which symbolized strength and endurance to him. Examining the Frieze adorned with the names of the 72 engineers, scientists, and industrialists who contributed to the tower's creation, Mark reflected on their lasting influence and the historical context of their work.

This experience served as a moment of clarity for Mark, illustrating the power of human ingenuity and collaboration across generations. It reminded him of the importance of perseverance and foresight, aligning with the themes of personal development and discovery central to his own voyage.

The most interesting moment came as Mark stood on the second floor of the Eiffel Tower, overlooking the twinkling city lights. Night time, indeed, was the right time. Although he wasn't allowed to get to the top of the tower, the panoramic view he got from the second floor was breathtaking. It was a combination of human achievement and natural beauty. It was here, on one of the world's most iconic landmarks, that Mark experienced a significant sense of clarity. He understood that his journey was not about reaching a final destination, but about embracing each step with intention and gratitude.

In that moment, Mark vowed to carry forward the lessons of his journey which includes facing challenges with courage, appreciating the beauty in every experience, and building a life that honored his past while embracing the future.

Paris had not only offered moments of clarity but had also reignited Mark's passion for life. The city's blend of history, art, and everyday wonder had provided a space for deep reflection and growth.

Leaving Paris, Mark carried with him the lessons learned in the City of Light. The memories of strolling along the Seine, the conversations with kindred spirits, and the awe-inspiring moments at the Eiffel Tower became part of his internal landscape. They were reminders that even in the face of loss and uncertainty, life was filled with beauty and potential.

Lessons from the Past

Throughout his journey, Mark encountered places where history had left indelible marks on the landscape and its people. In Athens, he climbed the Acropolis and stood in awe before the Parthenon. The Parthenon's majestic columns, though aged by time, still conveyed a sense of magnificence and timeless beauty. As Mark listened to the stories of ancient gods and philosophers, he gleaned timeless lessons about the pursuit of wisdom, the courage to question tradition, and the flexibility needed to navigate the storms of life.

As he wandered through the Agora, the heart of ancient Athens, Mark imagined the very busy marketplace filled with merchants, philosophers, and citizens engaging in lively debates. He could almost hear the echoes of Socrates questioning the status quo and urging his fellow Athenians to seek truth and knowledge. The ruins of the Stoa of Attalos, once a teeming colonnade where people gathered to discuss politics and philosophy, reminded Mark of the importance of dialogue and the exchange of ideas in fostering personal and societal growth.

One evening, as the sun set behind the Acropolis, casting a golden glow over the city, Mark sat on a quiet hill overlooking the ancient ruins. He reflected on the teachings of the philosophers who once roamed these streets like Plato, Aristotle, and Epicurus, to name but a few. Their ideas about ethics, happiness, and the nature of the universe meant a lot to him. He realized that the pursuit of wisdom was not just an intellectual exercise but a lifelong adventure that required humility, curiosity, and an open mind.

The lessons of Athens were not confined to the past. As Mark observed modern Athenians navigating their daily lives amidst economic challenges and social upheaval, he saw the same courageous spirit that had defined their ancestors. The graffiti-covered walls and the colorful street art told stories of protest, hope, and a relentless desire for change. In these expressions of contemporary life, Mark found inspiration to face his own challenges with firmness and determination.

Walking through the narrow streets of Jerusalem's Old City, Mark felt the weight of centuries-old conflicts and the enduring hope for peace that echoed in the prayers of pilgrims at the Western Wall. The city's labyrinthine alleys, filled with the mingling aromas of spices and the strains of sacred chants, offered a sensory journey through time. In the Jewish Quarter, he watched families light Shabbat candles with their faces illuminated with a serene glow that spoke of tradition and continuity.

At the Western Wall, Mark placed his hand on the ancient stones, feeling the vibrations of countless prayers that had been uttered over millennia. The Wall, a remnant of the Second Temple, stood as a symbol of faith and resilience. Here, amidst the murmurs of prayer and the quiet sobs of those seeking solace, Mark witnessed the power of faith to sustain and transform lives. He felt a deep sense of connection to something greater than himself, inspiring him to embrace a deeper sense of spirituality and compassion in his own journey.

Exploring the Christian Quarter, Mark visited the Church of the Holy Sepulchre, believed to be the site of Jesus' crucifixion and resurrection. The dimly lit interior, filled with the scent of incense and the flicker of candles, evoked a sense of reverence and awe. He watched as pilgrims from around the world knelt in prayer, their faces etched with devotion and hope. The church's age-old stones bore witness to the enduring power of faith and the human longing for redemption and grace.

In the Muslim Quarter, Mark strolled through the bustling souks, where merchants hawked spices, textiles, and intricate handicrafts. The call to prayer echoed through the narrow streets, creating a rhythmic backdrop to the vibrant life of the city. At the Dome of the Rock, he marveled at the golden dome that shimmered against the blue sky, a symbol of Islamic heritage and spirituality. Here, he learned about the principles of faith, charity, and community that guided the lives of millions around the world.

The stories of Athens and Jerusalem, though rooted in the past, offered timeless lessons that transcended historical boundaries. They taught Mark about the flexible and resilient nature of the human spirit, the enduring quest for knowledge and meaning, and the transformative power of faith and compassion. These lessons, interwoven with his personal reflections and experiences, became a source of fortitude and motivation as he continued his journey.

As Mark moved forward, the lessons from Athens and Jerusalem remained engraved in his heart and mind. They shaped his understanding of the world and his place within it, guiding him to embrace the wisdom of the past while forging a path toward a more enlightened and compassionate future.

Discoveries in Unexpected Places

Some of the most incredible discoveries came in unanticipated places. Mark once had a chance encounter with a nomadic family in the Moroccan desert, sharing a meal under a starlit sky and listening to their stories of perseverance in the face of adversity.

Mark's trip through Morocco began in the bustling medina of Marrakech, where the beautiful catchy colors and chaotic energy of the souks charmed his senses. The scent of cinnamon, cumin, and saffron filled the air, mingling with the sound of merchandisers calling out their wares and the distant rhythm of Gnawa music. It was in this lively atmosphere that Mark met Ali, a local guide with deep roots in the Sahara Desert.

Ali's rough, weather-beaten face and kind eyes spoke of a life spent navigating the vast dunes and remote oases of the desert. Intrigued by Ali's stories, Mark decided to embark on a trip into the heart of the Sahara. They set off in a sturdy 4x4, leaving behind the crowded streets of Marrakech for the serene, endless expanse of sand.

As they traveled deeper into the desert, the landscape transformed into a mesmerizing sea of golden dunes, undulating under the intense blue sky. The silence of the Sahara was extreme, broken only by the soft whisper of the wind. It was in this otherworldly setting that Mark first encountered the nomadic family who would leave an indelible mark on his journey.

The family's encampment was a simple yet welcoming collection of tents, nestled in the shelter of a large dune. They greeted Mark with warm smiles and gestures. Their hospitality immediately put him at ease. That evening, as the sun dipped below the horizon, the night sky was seen glowing with countless stars.

Under the vast starlit canopy, Mark sat around a fire with the family, sharing a meal of tagine, a savory stew of meat and vegetables slow-cooked in a clay pot. The aroma of cumin and coriander filled the air, mingling with the sweet scent of mint tea. The family's matriarch, Aicha, served the tea with practiced grace, pouring it from high above the glasses to create a frothy top.

As they ate and drank, Ali translated the family's stories for Mark. He learned of their nomadic heritage, a way of life passed down through generations. They spoke of the challenges they faced such as droughts, sandstorms, and the ever encroaching pressures of modernity. Yet, there was power in their words, a steadfast determination to preserve their traditions and adapt to the changing world.

One of the most moving moments came when Aicha shared the story of her son, Karim, who had left the desert to seek work in the city. She spoke of her pride in his courage and her hope for his future, but also of the heartache of separation. Mark was struck by the universal nature of their experiences which had themes of love, sacrifice, and the pursuit of a better life.

As the night grew darker and the fire burned lower, the family sang traditional Berber songs, their voices blending harmoniously with the gentle rustle of the desert breeze. Mark felt an intense sense of connection to these strangers who had welcomed him into their lives with such open hearts. He realized that despite the vast differences in their backgrounds, they shared a common humanity, bound by the same hopes, dreams, and challenges.

The next morning, Mark accompanied the family on their daily routine. He helped tend to their herd of goats, learning how they sourced water from hidden wells and navigated the shifting sands. The simplicity and rhythm of their life offered a stark contrast to the fast-paced, technology driven world he had left behind.

Living among the nomads, Mark learned the art of patience and the value of simplicity. He observed how they cherished the little things. Things as little as a cool breeze on a hot day, the first sip of tea at dawn, the laughter of children playing in the sand. These moments of joy and contentment, often taken for granted in his own life, became precious lessons in gratitude and mindfulness.

As the days passed, Mark felt a deepening bond with the family. He admired their strength and adaptability, their ability to find beauty and meaning in the harshest of environments. Their stories of endurance and an ability to adapt freely inspired him to confront his own challenges with renewed courage and perspective.

When it was time to leave, Mark felt a mixture of gratitude and sadness. The family gathered to bid him farewell with their smiles and well-wishes. As he climbed back into the 4x4 with Ali, Mark carried with him not only memories of breathtaking landscapes and starlit nights but also a sincere appreciation for the lessons he had learned from his time with the nomads.

The experience in the Moroccan desert became a touchstone for Mark's journey, a reminder of the strength and power that resides within all of us. It reinforced his belief in the power of human connection to bridge divides and nurture understanding. These discoveries, found in the most unexpected of places, enriched his journey and deepened his sense of purpose, guiding him toward a future filled with hope and possibility.

After experiencing a series of lessons in unexpected places, Mark's journey in Marrakech continues to unfold. His encounters there, filled with resilience despite vulnerabilities, will be further explored in a later chapter of this book.

Mumbai, a city that never sleeps, welcomed Mark with its chaotic energy and an overwhelming sensory overload. As he stepped out of Chhatrapati Shivaji Maharaj International Airport, the humid air and loud noise enveloped him. The city's heartbeat could be felt in the constant honking of cars, the cries of street vendors, and the laughter of children playing cricket in the narrow lanes.

Mark's exploration of Mumbai began in Colaba, a bustling district known for its colonial architecture and vibrant street life. The Gateway of India, standing majestically by the Arabian Sea, was his first stop. As he gazed at the monumental arch, Mark couldn't help but think of the millions of travelers who had passed through it, each with their own story and purpose. Walking along the Colaba Causeway, Mark was struck by the sheer diversity of people and goods. Street vendors sold everything from intricately designed jewelry and traditional Indian textiles to the latest electronic gadgets. The aroma of freshly made pav bhaji, a spicy vegetable mash served with buttered bread, wafted through the air, mingling with the scent of incense from nearby temples. It was in this vibrant setting that Mark met Ravi, a local shopkeeper with a warm smile and an infectious enthusiasm for his city. Ravi invited Mark to explore Mumbai beyond the typical tourist spots, offering to show him the hidden gems and lesser-known aspects of the city. Intrigued by Ravi's offer, Mark eagerly accepted. Their first stop was Dhobi Ghat, the world's largest outdoor laundry. Mark watched in amazement as hundreds of dhobis (washermen) and women scrubbed, rinsed, and hung clothes to dry in an intricate ballet of movement. The sheer scale and efficiency of the operation were awe-inspiring, pointing to the industrious spirit of the city's inhabitants. From Dhobi Ghat, Ravi led Mark to the bustling Crawford Market, a sensory overload of colors, sounds, and smells. The market was a maze of narrow alleys lined with stalls selling fresh fruits and vegetables, aromatic spices, and exotic pets.

Mark marveled at the variety of produce, from piles of vibrant mangoes and pomegranates to stacks of fragrant coriander and cumin. As they navigated the crowded market, Ravi shared stories of Mumbai's history and its unique blend of cultures. He explained how the city had been shaped by waves of migration, from the Portuguese and British colonial periods to the influx of people from all over India seeking better opportunities. This rich blend of influences was evident in the city's diverse cuisine, architecture, and festivals. One evening, Ravi took Mark to experience the magic of a Bollywood movie at a local cinema. The film, filled with melodrama and elaborate dance sequences, and catchy songs, captivated Mark. He was struck by how Bollywood, with its larger-than-life stories and vibrant aesthetics, reflected the dreams and aspirations of millions of Indians. The communal experience of watching the film, with the audience cheering, laughing, and singing along, was unlike anything Mark had ever encountered.

Another unforgettable experience was a visit to the dabbawalas, Mumbai's legendary lunch delivery service. Mark watched in awe as hundreds of dabbawalas, dressed in white uniforms and traditional Gandhi caps, sorted and delivered thousands of lunchboxes with remarkable precision. Ravi explained the intricate coding system that ensured each lunchbox reached its intended recipient, emphasizing the efficiency and dedication of the dabbawalas. Mark's journey through Mumbai also brought him face to face with the city's contrasts. In the affluent neighborhood of Malabar Hill, he visited the beautiful Hanging Gardens. There he enjoyed panoramic views of the city's skyline and Marine Drive, often referred to as the Queen's Necklace due to its string of sparkling lights. Yet, just a short distance away, he encountered the stark realities of life in Dharavi, one of Asia's largest slums. Walking through Dharavi with a local guide, Mark was deeply moved by the resourcefulness of its residents. Despite the challenging living conditions, there was a palpable sense of community and entrepreneurial spirit. He visited small-scale industries where people made pottery, recycled plastic, and produced leather goods, all within the labyrinthine lanes of the slum. These interactions showed how determined the people are as they found ways to thrive despite the odds.

Mark also found solace in the serene Haji Ali Dargah, a mosque and tomb situated on an islet off the coast of Worli. This place was only accessible during low tide. The shrine stood as a symbol of faith and devotion, attracting pilgrims from all walks of life. As Mark walked along the causeway leading to the mosque, he felt a sense of peace amidst the rhythmic sound of waves and the distant call to prayer.

One of Mark's most heartwarming experiences was visiting a local NGO that worked with street children. Ravi introduced Mark to the organization, where he spent time interacting with the children, listening to their stories, and participating in educational activities. The children's zest for life, despite their circumstances, left a lasting impression on Mark's mind. Their laughter and dreams reminded him of the desire for a better future seen everywhere in the world.

As his time in Mumbai drew to a close, Mark reflected on the myriad of experiences that had enriched his understanding of the world and himself. The wide array of cultures in the city, its contrasts of wealth and poverty, and the indomitable spirit of its people had left an indelible mark on his heart. Mark realized that Mumbai was a living, breathing entity that embodied the complexities and beauty of human existence.

These discoveries in unexpected places, whether in the heart of the Moroccan desert or the streets of Mumbai, reinforced Mark's belief in the power of human connection. His journey through Mumbai had deepened his appreciation for the ingenuity of the human spirit. He found solace in the realization that life, much like his travels, was a journey filled with unexpected turns. His experiences helped him to heal the wounds left by his father's passing. He understood that his grief was a part of the larger human experience, shared by many across different cultures and backgrounds. The warmth and generosity he experienced in Mumbai and Morocco reminded him of his father's kindness and the enduring impact of human compassion. This understanding became a beacon of light, guiding him through the darkness of his loss and giving him the strength to move forward with renewed vigor and hope.

In the streets of Delhi, India, Mark's journey to Nepal began unexpectedly. Drawn by stories of spiritual awakening and breathtaking landscapes, he embarked on a train journey through the lush plains and winding rivers that eventually led him to the foothills of the Himalayas.

Arriving in Kathmandu, he was greeted by the chaotic charm of its markets, where traders adorned in colorful saris and turbans bartered over intricately woven fabrics and spices that filled the air with an exotic aroma. Here, Mark met Tenzin, a seasoned trekking guide with a kind of hilarious laugh and a deep knowledge of the mountains. Over steaming cups of masala chai, Tenzin shared tales of his daring climbs and encounters with elusive snow leopards. Each story was crafted with reverence for the rugged beauty that surrounded them.

Together, they ventured into the serene valleys and terraced hillsides, where prayer flags fluttered in the mountain breeze and monasteries clung to the cliff sides like ancient sentinels. At a remote monastery high above a mist-shrouded valley, Mark joined monks in their daily rituals, chanting mantras as the sun painted the peaks in hues of gold and crimson. The stillness of the mountains and the rhythmic prayers became a gateway to understanding the important teachings of Tibetan Buddhism. Lessons of temporariness, compassion, and the relation of all living beings.

During treks through rhododendron forests ablaze with blooms and encounters with yak herders tending their high altitude pastures, Mark learned the need to be adaptable from the Sherpa communities, who thrived amidst the harsh conditions of the Himalayan slopes. Nights spent around crackling fires were filled with laughter and stories that bridged cultures and generations, revealing the universal joys of human connection and the tenacity forged through shared hardships.

In Kathmandu's ancient temples and stupas, Mark marveled at intricate wood carvings depicting gods and goddesses, while Tenzin explained the symbolism behind each detail. To Mark, these were lessons of spirituality and devotion that transcended language and culture. Together, they explored the markets of Thamel, where the aroma of steaming momos and the vibrant colors of prayer flags adorned every corner, immersing Mark in the richness of Nepalese culture and tradition.

He joined locals in planting rice paddies, their rhythmic movements synchronized with ancient agricultural rituals that honored the land and its abundance. Working side by side with farmers, he learned the patience required to nurture crops from seedling to harvest, a lesson in perseverance mirrored in the towering mountains that framed their daily toil.

One memorable evening, Mark was invited to a traditional Nepali feast, where he sat cross-legged on a mat, surrounded by smiling faces and the aromatic scent of dal bhat wafting from large metal plates. Over hearty servings of rice, lentils, and spiced vegetables, elders shared stories that had passed down through generations. Each story carried with it the endurance of families rebuilding homes shattered by seismic tremors, the endurance of farmers persevering through biting cold to protect their livestock, and the steadfastness of communities navigating turbulent political changes with unwavering unity. These narratives not only shaped their collective memory but also embodied the unwritten codes of strength and solidarity that bound them together, overpassing time and adversity.

In Pokhara, nestled beside the serene Phewa Lake with the Annapurna Range looming in the distance, Mark found solace in the tranquility of nature. Early mornings were spent paddling a wooden boat across the calm waters, the sun rising over snow-capped peaks mirrored in the lake's surface. Here, he met Pasang, a local fisherman whose old weak hands deftly maneuvered the boat, and whose laughter could be heard in the quiet moments, interrupted only by the occasional sound of an oar splashing in the water.

They hiked through dense forests filled with colorful blooms, stopping at secluded spots to admire golden eagles soaring high in the sky. Pasang's quiet reverence for the mountains and deep connection to the land spoke volumes about resilience in the face of natural beauty and hardship alike. As they huddled around a campfire under a star-strewn sky, sharing stories of mountain legends and the spirits that guarded their peaks, Mark felt a profound sense of belonging, a moment where cultural boundaries dissolved, leaving only the shared humanity beneath.

In the noisy busy streets of Kathmandu's Thamel district, Mark experienced the pulse of city life mingled with ancient traditions. He wandered through narrow alleys lined with prayer wheels and colorful storefronts selling handcrafted artifacts. Each piece told a story of skilled craftsmanship passed down through centuries. Here, he met Sita, a skilled artisan renowned for her intricate wood carvings adorning temple doors and rooftops. Her craftsmanship reflected a deep cultural heritage and also demonstrated a seamless blend of traditional artistry with contemporary influences, captivating Mark with each detail she meticulously carved.

Mark spent time observing her work, discussing the intricate details of the wood carvings and the stories they conveyed about Nepal's rich artistic traditions. Sita, in turn, shared details about her creative process, describing the symbolism behind each motif and the techniques. They bonded over a mutual love for art and history, exchanging stories that enriched Mark's understanding of Nepalese culture and left a lasting impression on his adventure.

Mark's travel from India to Nepal wasn't just a physical passage but a soul-stirring adventure, where every encounter, whether with a mountain peak or a humble monk, revealed a deeper understanding of life's mysteries and the enduring spirit of exploration that defines his path.

Personal Growth and Transformation

Reflecting on his journey thus far, Mark realized that each experience he had, either joyful or challenging, had contributed to his understanding of life and the need to remain strong despite life's challenges.

Mark began to unravel the layers of grief that had initially propelled him on this odyssey. He discovered that healing was a collage of experiences, and not just a straightforward path. Each fragment of the healing process contributes to a larger picture of acceptance and renewal. Embracing the lessons of his travels, Mark cultivated a deeper sense of gratitude for the preciousness of life and the enduring bonds of love that transcended physical separation.

Chapter 4: Resilience in Adversity

In the depths of his journey, Mark Reynolds encountered trials that tested his resolve and his understanding of resilience in the face of adversity. From the loud streets of Tokyo to the quieter landscapes, each experience demonstrated the human spirit's capacity to endure and grow amidst life's challenges.

Challenges and Growth

Tokyo greeted Mark with its neon-lit streets and bustling crowds, a stark contrast to the quietness he had found in smaller towns and remote villages. The city's fast-paced energy was overwhelming, presenting a new set of challenges that tested Mark's flexibility and strength. Navigating the intricate cultural nuances and language barriers of Tokyo, Mark learned to thrive in these unfamiliar surroundings, finding growth in the discomfort and excitement of his new environment.

Upon arriving in Tokyo, Mark was immediately struck by the magnitude of the city. The tall skyscrapers, the endless flow of people, and the vibrant street life created an overwhelming sight, one more than the brain can process. His initial days were spent simply acclimating to the rhythm of Tokyo, which moved at a pace he had never experienced before. Simple tasks like ordering food or asking for directions required effort and patience, pushing Mark to step out of his comfort zone and engage with the local culture more deeply.

Mark's journey through Tokyo was marked by a series of cultural encounters that enriched his understanding of Japanese society. He frequented traditional izakayas, small pubs where locals gathered after work to unwind and also socialize. In these cozy establishments, Mark learned the unspoken rules of Japanese etiquette, from the proper way to pour drinks for others to the significance of different seating arrangements. Each evening spent in an izakaya taught humility and respect, reinforcing the importance of observing and honoring cultural traditions.

In contrast to the lively nightlife, Mark found comfort in the serene environment of Tokyo's ancient temples and gardens. Places like the Meiji Shrine and Senso-ji Temple offered a peaceful respite from the city's chaos. Walking through these sacred grounds, Mark practiced mindfulness and reflection, drawing parallels between the physical journey he was on and his inner path of healing. The tranquility of these spaces provided a counterbalance to the intensity of urban life, reminding him of the value of balance and harmony.

One of the most impactful experiences in Tokyo was Mark's encounter with Hiroshi, a seasoned businessman who had spent decades navigating Japan's corporate landscape. They met by chance in a tucked-away noodle shop, where Hiroshi's warm demeanor and open curiosity led to a meaningful conversation over steaming bowls of ramen.

Hiroshi shared stories of his career, detailing the pressures of success and the sacrifices he had made along the way. He spoke candidly about the highs and lows, the moments of triumph and the setbacks that had tested his resolve. For Mark, Hiroshi's narrative was a revelation. It highlighted the universal struggle for balance amidst life's demands and the importance of perseverance during periods of adversity.

As they went deeper in their conversation, Hiroshi imparted wisdom that meant a lot to Mark. He emphasized the importance of maintaining a sense of balance in work, and all aspects of life. Hiroshi's advice was to embrace challenges as opportunities for growth, to view setbacks not as failures, but as stepping stones towards personal development. This perspective was a transformative one for Mark, reinforcing the power inherent in embracing life's challenges with an open heart and a determined spirit.

The city's dynamic environment pushed him to develop new skills and adapt quickly to changing circumstances. He learned to navigate the intricacies of urban life, from mastering the Tokyo Metro system to understanding the nuances of Japanese social interactions. Each new experience, whether it was a simple exchange with a local shopkeeper or a deeper conversation with a newfound friend, contributed to his evolving understanding of strength in misfortunes.

Mark's journaling practice became even more important during his time in Tokyo.

Each night, he would document his experiences, reflecting on the lessons learned and the emotions felt throughout the day. This process of introspection helped him make sense of his journey, allowing him to identify patterns and insights that might have otherwise gone unnoticed.

Tokyo also offered Mark the chance to build meaningful connections with people from diverse backgrounds. He joined a language exchange group, where he met locals and expatriates who were eager to share their experiences and learn from each other. These interactions broadened Mark's viewpoint, allowing him to see the world through different lenses and appreciate the richness of cultural diversity.

One particularly memorable connection was with a young artist named Aiko. They met at a gallery showcasing her work, and Mark was immediately drawn to the emotional depth and vibrant colors of her paintings. Through their conversations, Aiko shared her own way of healing through art, describing how her creative process had helped her navigate personal challenges and express her innermost thoughts. Inspired by her story, Mark began to explore his own creative outlets, finding solace and expression through writing and photography.

The process of self-discovery also involved transforming pain into purpose. Mark's experiences in various cities had taught him that pain, while inevitable, could be a catalyst for growth and change. It was in Kyoto, which was a blend of Gothic architecture and modernist marvels, that he began to channel his pain into creative expression. He attended a workshop on storytelling, where participants were encouraged to share their personal narratives through various art forms.

Mark chose to write, pouring his emotions into words that captured his journey, his struggles, and his triumphs. The act of writing became therapeutic, a way to process his feelings and make sense of his experiences. He wrote about the loss of his father, the impact it had on his family, and the lessons he had learned along the way. Through his writing, he discovered a newfound sense of purpose which is to share his story with others who might be going through similar struggles.

In Kyoto, Mark explored the world of art and found inspiration in the masterpieces of the Renaissance. The works of Michelangelo, Leonardo da Vinci, and Botticelli spoke to him on a deep level. Their timeless beauty and profound messages touched him deeply as he went through his own journey of recuperation. He spent hours in the Uffizi Gallery, contemplating the intricate details and the emotions captured in the paintings. The experience ignited a passion for art and a desire to create something meaningful.

Volunteering was another avenue through which Mark found strength in Tokyo. He joined a local nonprofit organization that provided support to the city's homeless population, participating in outreach programs and community events. These experiences were eye-opening, showing the stark contrast between Tokyo's affluence and the struggles faced by its most vulnerable residents.

Through his volunteer work, Mark gained a deeper appreciation for the power of togetherness and collective action. He witnessed firsthand the impact of grassroots efforts to address social issues and support those in need. This involvement not only enriched his understanding of social justice but also reinforced his belief in the importance of giving back and supporting others on their own journeys.

Ultimately, Mark's time in Tokyo showed the transformative power of embracing challenges. He encountered many obstacles. For example, he was faced with language barriers, cultural differences, and moments of personal doubt. But all these obstacles became an opportunity for him to grow and re-discover himself. He navigated the struggles of urban life, emerging with a deeper understanding of himself and the world around him.

Overcoming Obstacles

Tokyo's beautiful cityscape, with its well lit busy streets, presented a vastly different backdrop for Mark's journey. The urban jungle, with its beautiful skyscrapers and ceaseless activity, was a far cry from the serene mountains he had traversed earlier in his travels. Yet, amidst the chaos of the city, Mark found new challenges and opportunities to test his resilience and adaptability.

From the moment he arrived, Tokyo's overwhelming energy was palpable. The large number of people, the constant noise, and the rapid pace of life were both thrilling and intimidating. Mark quickly realized that thriving in this environment would require a different kind of resilience than what he had developed in slower, more isolated places. The first obstacle was simply finding his way around the sprawling metropolis. The labyrinthine subway system, with its myriad lines and stations, was a puzzle he had to solve daily. Each journey required careful planning and quick thinking, especially when language barriers added to the complexity.

One of the unique aspects of Tokyo was its seamless integration of advanced technology into everyday life. From high-speed trains to automated convenience stores, the city's technological prowess was a marvel. At the same time, it posed a challenge. Mark, who had always been more comfortable with nature than gadgets, had to learn to navigate this high-tech landscape. He struggled initially with everything from using vending machines to managing cashless payments. However, with each small victory, whether successfully ordering food via a touchscreen menu or navigating his way using a GPS app, Mark's confidence grew.

Despite the crowds, Tokyo offered pockets of tranquility where Mark could find respite from the fast and energetic pace. He discovered hidden gardens and quiet temples, places where he could reflect and recharge. One such sanctuary was the Shinjuku Gyoen National Garden, a vast green oasis in the heart of the city. Mark found a semblance of the peace he had experienced in nature as he walked through its manicured landscapes. These moments of solitude were crucial for maintaining his mental well-being amidst the relentless urban hustle.

Tokyo's streets were a melting pot of humanity with each person navigating their own challenges and triumphs. Mark often found inspiration in observing the daily lives of the city's residents. The stoic determination of office workers, the creative energy of street performers, and the meticulous craftsmanship of shopkeepers all offered Mark informal lessons in perseverance and dedication.

One particularly inspiring encounter was with an elderly street vendor named Yuki. Despite her age, Yuki operated a small food stall with remarkable vigor and cheerfulness. Over several visits, Mark learned about her life. He learnt how she had rebuilt her business after losing everything in a natural disaster, and how she found joy in serving her customers. Yuki's story was a reminder that resilience was not just about overcoming great obstacles but also about finding strength in everyday challenges and continuing to move forward with optimism.

As said earlier, there were moments of loneliness and self-doubt, especially when he struggled with the language or felt disconnected from the local culture. However, these challenges forced him to develop new coping strategies. He took up meditation to calm his mind, practiced a few Japanese diligently, and made an effort to connect with locals and fellow travelers. Each of these steps, though small, helped him build a stronger sense of resilience, making it easier for him to adjust to changing circumstances.

Mark had an unexpected encounter with Satoshi, a retired samurai swordsmith. He met Satoshi in a small workshop tucked away in a quiet alley, where the master craftsman was demonstrating his art. Intrigued by the meticulous process of forging swords, Mark struck up a conversation with Satoshi, who welcomed him into his world with open arms.

Satoshi's life story was one of great honor coupled with tremendous hardship. He spoke of the discipline and patience required to master his craft, and how each sword reflected the resilient, balanced, and unwavering samurai spirit. Throughout his stay, Satoshi shared his touching experiences with Mark. He explained that true strength came not from avoiding difficulties but from facing them head-on and learning to bend without breaking. Mark saw parallels in his own journey of navigating life's challenges and never took these experiences shared for granted.

Tokyo also taught Mark the importance of balance and harmony in life. The city's culture of mindfulness and respect, offered valuable insights into maintaining equilibrium amidst chaos. Mark began to incorporate these principles into his daily routine. He practiced mindfulness, taking moments to breathe and center himself even in the busiest of settings. He also embraced the concept of "wa," the Japanese notion of harmony, in his interactions with others, striving to create positive and balanced relationships.

As Mark's time in Tokyo drew to a close, he took the opportunity to reflect on the obstacles he had overcome and the growth he had experienced. The city's dynamic environment had pushed him to his limits, but it had also shown him the depths of his strength and the capacity for continuous adjustment. He realized that each challenge, whether it was navigating a new subway route or overcoming a moment of self-doubt, had contributed to his personal transformation.

The lessons learned from the city's streets, its people, and its culture had enriched his journey and deepened his understanding of resilience. As he prepared to leave, Mark carried with him a renewed sense of strength and an appreciation for the journey itself, the continuous process of facing challenges, learning, and evolving.

In the end, Tokyo was not just a city of obstacles but a place of hope. It was more like a school to him. Mark left Tokyo with a heart full of gratitude and a spirit fortified by the lessons he had learned, ready to continue his quest with all determination.

Finding Strength in Vulnerability

In the labyrinthine streets of Marrakech's medina, amidst the cultural richness, Mark encountered individuals whose resilience was forged in the crucible of history and tradition, exploring centuries-old alleys with grace and fortitude.

One transformative experience was with Fatima, a local artisan whose intricate designs adorned handcrafted pottery and textiles. In her modest workshop tucked away from the main square, Fatima shared the story of how she overcame personal loss and economic hardship through creativity and tenacity. Her courage and strength shone through in the meticulous craftsmanship of each piece, confirming the transformative power of vulnerability and the strength found in embracing one's authentic self.

Mark was drawn to the colors and patterns in Fatima's work. Each design told a story of its own. Sitting in her workshop, he listened to Fatima recount the challenges she faced after losing her husband who was the primary breadwinner of the family. Left with little more than her skills and an unwavering spirit, she turned to her art as a means of survival and expression. She explained how each brushstroke and stitch was imbued with her emotions, turning pain into beauty.

Mark watched Fatima's deft hands transform raw materials into exquisite works of art. The intricacy of her designs mirrored the complexity of her life, a dance between sorrow and hope, struggle and triumph. Fatima's story resonated deeply with Mark, reminding him of his own life.

The time spent in Fatima's workshop was more than a lesson in artistry but also in the strength that comes from vulnerability. She spoke of the support she received from the local community. She recounted how neighbors rallied around her during her toughest times, offering both financial assistance and emotional support. She explained how this was useful to her at that point in time and how she found strength in unity and shared experiences.

Inspired by Fatima's story, Mark reflected on his own susceptibility. He realized that in trying to be strong for everyone else, he had often overlooked the power of showing his true self. In the heart of Marrakech, surrounded by the hum of the medina and the warmth of human connection, he began to understand that true strength lay in acknowledging and embracing his weaknesses.

Fatima invited Mark to try his hand at pottery, guiding him through the delicate process of shaping clay. As he worked, he found the experience meditative, each movement requiring focus and care. The clay, malleable yet resistant, became an analogy for his own life, in that it is shaped by external forces yet holding the potential for beauty and strength. The act of creating something tangible from a simple lump of clay was therapeutic, representing how vulnerability can lead to immense change.

Throughout his travels, Mark had often encountered individuals like Fatima, who despite facing tremendous adversity, found ways to channel their struggles into something meaningful. These encounters underscored the universal truth that vulnerability, far from being a weakness, is a source of massive strength. It is through acknowledging it, that we find our true selves and connect more deeply with others.

Mark's time in Marrakech, particularly his experience with Fatima, became a pivotal moment in his journey of self-discovery. He began to see his own grief not as a burden to be hidden. Rather he started seeing it as a part of his story that could inspire others, providing consolation and encouragement to those on similar paths.

As Mark continued his journey, the lessons from Fatima stayed with him. Each new place he got to offered fresh perspectives, but the core lesson remained the same, that strength is found not in the absence of hardship, but in the courage to face it head-on and emerge stronger, wiser, and more compassionate.

Mark's time in Marrakech continued to unfold in unexpected ways. Each day, he found new opportunities to connect with the locals and learn from their experiences. One morning, while wandering through the medina, he met Ahmed, an elderly man who owned a small spice shop. The very beautiful colors and intoxicating aromas drew Mark in, but it was Ahmed's warmth and willingness to share his knowledge that kept him there for hours.

Ahmed had been running the spice shop for decades, a family business passed down through generations. He shared stories of how his grandfather had traveled across continents, seeking the finest spices to bring back to Marrakech. As Mark listened, he was struck by the dedication and passion that had sustained Ahmed's family through changing times and economic challenges.

One day, Ahmed invited Mark to join him on a trip to the Atlas Mountains, where some of the spices were sourced. This journey into the heart of Morocco's natural beauty was another eye-opener for Mark. The rugged landscape and the bravery of the people who lived there were humbling and to a large extent, inspiring. Mark watched as Ahmed negotiated with local farmers, demonstrating a deep respect for their hard work and knowledge.

During this excursion, Mark had the chance to meet Amina, a young woman who worked with her family to harvest saffron, one of the most precious spices in the world. Amina's hands bore the marks of years of labor, yet her eyes sparkled with pride as she explained the painstaking process of cultivating and harvesting saffron threads. She spoke of the joy and sense of purpose she found in continuing her family's legacy.

Through these interactions, Mark began to understand the deep connections between people and their land. The resilience of these communities was rooted in their relationship with nature and their commitment to preserving their heritage.

He saw parallels to his own journey, realizing that his search for healing was also about finding and nurturing his own roots.

Back in Marrakech, Mark's experiences with Fatima, Ahmed, and Amina led him to a new project. He started the task of documenting the stories of the artisans and farmers he had met. He wanted to create a platform where their voices could be heard and their resilience celebrated. He spent days interviewing them, taking photographs, and writing their stories, feeling a sense of purpose and fulfillment he hadn't experienced in a long time.

The process of creating this project was soothing to Mark. As he pieced together the narratives, he found himself reflecting on his own story. He realized that, just like the people he was documenting, his resilience was built on the connections he had made and the lessons he had learned along the way. This project became a way for him to honor those connections and contribute something meaningful to the world.

One evening, while reviewing his notes and photographs in a quiet café, Mark met Leila, a journalist who was intrigued by his project. Leila had spent years covering stories of empowerment across Africa, and she offered to help Mark amplify the voices of the people he had met. Together, they brainstormed ideas for a book and a series of articles that would reach a wider audience.

Collaborating with Leila brought a new dimension to Mark's journey. Her insights and experiences enriched the project, and her enthusiasm was contagious. They spent late nights working together, fueled by a shared passion for storytelling and a belief in the power of teamwork.

As the project gained momentum, Mark felt a sense of fulfillment. The stories he had collected showed the strength of the human spirit, and sharing them with the world was a way to honor the people who had touched his life. He realized that his journey was not just about finding healing for himself but about contributing to a larger narrative of endurance and hope.

Mark's days in Marrakech were filled with moments that would etch themselves into his memory forever. One morning, he was invited to a local wedding by Youssef, a young man he had met at a community event. The invitation was a great honor, and Mark was excited at this offer. More importantly, he was curious about the cultural significance of the occasion.

The wedding was a beautiful celebration of love and community, held in a beautifully decorated courtyard filled with music, laughter, and the aroma of delicious food. Mark was welcomed with open arms by Youssef's family, who treated him as one of their own. He observed the intricate rituals and traditions which carried deep meanings that spoke to the values and history of the community.

As he watched the bride and groom exchange vows, surrounded by their loved ones, Mark was struck by the joy that permeated the event. Despite the hardships many faced, moments of celebration and unity brought a sense of hope and continuity. It reminded Mark of the importance of cherishing life's joyous occasions, no matter how fleeting they might be.

In the days following the wedding, Mark had the opportunity to visit a local school where children from underprivileged backgrounds were receiving education and support. The school, run by an NGO, aimed to provide not just academic knowledge but also life skills and emotional support. Mark spent time with the children, listening to their stories and participating in their activities.

One of the children, a bright-eyed girl named Nadia, particularly touched Mark's heart. Despite her young age, Nadia had already faced significant challenges. Her parents had passed away, and she was being raised by her grandmother. Yet, her spirit was unbroken, and she approached life with an infectious enthusiasm and a desire to learn.

Nadia's favorite subject was art, and she eagerly showed Mark her drawings and paintings. Through her art, Nadia expressed her dreams and aspirations, creating vivid depictions of a world filled with beauty and possibility. Mark was inspired by her creativity, seeing in her a reflection of the strength and hope that characterized so many of the people he had met in Marrakech.

Moved by his experiences at the school, Mark decided to contribute in a meaningful way. He organized a small fundraiser among his friends back home, raising funds to support the school's programs and provide resources for the children. The response was overwhelming, and Mark felt fulfilled knowing he was making a tangible difference in the lives of these children.

One evening in Marrakech, Mark attended a traditional music performance in the Jemaa el-Fna square, a lively and bustling center of activity. The square was a sensory feast, with musicians, dancers, and storytellers captivating the crowds. Mark found a spot among the spectators, losing himself in the rhythm and energy of the performance.

As he listened to the haunting melodies of the oud and the rhythmic beats of the darbuka, Mark felt a profound connection to the culture and history of Morocco. The music spoke of bravery, of joy and sorrow, of triumphs and struggles. It demonstrated the power of art and tradition to convey the deepest human emotions and experiences.

Reflecting on his time in Marrakech, Mark realized how much he had grown and learned. The city had challenged him, inspired him, and shown him the strength of the human spirit in ways he had never imagined. The people he had met, from Fatima to Ahmed, Amina to Nadia, had each taught him invaluable lessons about resilience, hope, and the power of connection that he decided to stay even longer in Marrakech. He knew that his search for recuperation was far from over.

As the days in Marrakech stretched on, Mark became more attuned to the rhythms of the city and the intricacies of its culture. He began to rise early, joining the locals in their morning routines. One particularly memorable morning, Mark found himself at a small bakery tucked away in a narrow alley, drawn by the tantalizing aroma of freshly baked bread.

The baker, an elderly man named Hassan, greeted Mark with a warm smile and invited him to help knead the dough. As they worked side by side, Hassan shared stories of his family and the traditions passed down through generations. These customs were deeply embedded in his everyday routine, with each loaf of bread symbolizing the lasting heritage of his forebears. Mark listened intently.

Hassan began his tale by recounting the origins of his craft. His great-grandfather had opened the bakery in a small, sun-drenched village nestled in the hills. Back then, bread meant more than just a staple food. It was a symbol of sustenance and togetherness. The process of baking was deeply rooted in the rhythms of rural life, with each family contributing to the collective effort of kneading, baking, and sharing the bread. Festivals and celebrations revolved around the communal oven, where people gathered to bake, tell stories, and strengthen bonds.

Mark listened intently as Hassan described the early mornings when he would accompany his grandfather to the bakery. The elder would tell him that making bread was more of a calling than a job. He learned to treat each step of the process with reverence, from selecting the finest grains to nurturing the sourdough starter, which had been passed down for over a century. "This starter," Hassan explained, pointing to a bubbling jar of dough, "carries the essence of those who came before us. It connects us to our past and sustains us in the present."

As they continued to knead the dough, Hassan explained how each generation had added their unique touch to the family tradition. His grandmother, for instance, introduced a special blend of herbs that gave the bread its distinctive flavor, a secret recipe cherished and guarded over the years. His father, on the other hand, had modernized the bakery, introducing innovative techniques while maintaining the soul of the craft.

Hassan's own contribution was a renewed emphasis on togetherness. He organized baking workshops for local children, teaching them how to bake. He also taught them the values of patience, dedication, and collaboration. "Bread," he said, "is a metaphor for life. It requires time, effort, and love to transform simple ingredients into something nourishing and beautiful. Just like in life, we must be patient, work hard, and support each other."

Mark found parallels between Hassan's stories and his own journey. The act of kneading dough mirrored the process of working through his grief and finding new purpose. The way Hassan honored his ancestors was similar to Mark's efforts to keep his father's memory alive. The community spirit that infused the bakery reminded him of the importance of reconnecting with his family and building new traditions.

One particular story stayed with Mark long after he left the bakery. Hassan spoke of a time when a severe drought had struck the village, leaving many without food. The villagers, despite their own struggles, came together at the bakery. They pooled their resources, shared what little they had, and baked bread for everyone. "It was in those moments of hardship," Hassan said, "that we truly understood the power of unity and compassion."

Through these shared experiences, Mark realized that traditions were not just about preserving the past but about creating continuity and meaning in the present. They were about forging connections, giving him memories that provide strength and solace. As Mark's hands worked the dough, he experienced a deep sense of belonging, knowing that he was part of a larger story, a story that included his father, his family, and now, the lessons learned from a humble baker in a faraway land.

Hassan's parting words echoed in Mark's mind as he continued his journey: "Every loaf of bread tells a story. It speaks of the hands that kneaded it, the hearts that cherished it, and the community that shared it. Your story, too, is like bread. It is nourishing, sustaining, and filled with love. Never forget that."

The act of baking bread became a meditative experience for Mark, a moment of calm amidst the bustling city. It reminded him of the simple yet profound joys that could be found in everyday activities, and the ways in which these moments could foster a deeper understanding of oneself and others.

In the afternoons, Mark often wandered through the city's many museums and galleries, eager to immerse himself in Morocco's rich artistic heritage. One gallery, in particular, captivated his attention. It featured contemporary art created by young

Moroccan artists who used their work to address social issues and challenge conventional narratives.

Mark struck up a conversation with Layla, a young artist whose paintings depicted the struggles and triumphs of women in Moroccan society. Layla's art was bold and unapologetic, reflecting her own journey of empowerment and resistance. She spoke passionately about the importance of using art as a tool for social change, and her words touched Mark's heart deeply.

Inspired by Layla's courage and creativity, Mark decided to collaborate with her on a community art project. Together, they organized a single day workshop for local youth, encouraging them to express their thoughts and dreams through art. The workshops were a resounding success, and Mark was moved by the creativity and resilience of the young participants.

Through this project, Mark witnessed firsthand the power of art to inspire and transform. The children's artworks were displayed in a public exhibition, drawing crowds from across the city and sparking meaningful conversations about the future of their community. This experience reinforced Mark's belief in the potential of individuals to create positive change, regardless of their circumstances.

Evenings in Marrakech were a time for reflection and connection. Mark often found himself at a small café overlooking the bustling Jemaa el-Fnaa square, where he would sip mint tea and watch the world go by. The square was a simulation of the entire Marrakech, alive with energy and diversity, where musicians, performers, and merchants came together.

One evening, Mark struck up a conversation with Samir, a street musician whose soulful melodies had caught his ear. Samir shared his journey of pursuing music against the odds, his struggles with poverty, and his unwavering dedication to his craft. His music was not just a form of expression but a source of healing and hope.

Listening to Samir play, Mark felt uplifted. The music spoke to the universal human experience, transcending language and cultural barriers. It underscored the strength of determination and the value of pursuing one's passions despite facing hardship.

As his time in Marrakech drew to a close, Mark was invited to a traditional Moroccan feast at the home of Amina, a friend he had made during his stay. The evening was filled with laughter, stories, and an array of delicious dishes that showcased the richness of Moroccan cuisine. Mark felt a deep sense of belonging as he shared this special meal with Amina's family.

During the feast, Amina's grandmother recounted tales of their family's history, bringing together memories of triumph and trials. Mark was humbled by the honor of being included in such an intimate gathering.

As Mark continued his journey through Marrakech, he became more deeply embedded in the city's lifestyle. One day, while wandering through the narrow streets of the medina, he stumbled upon a small workshop that specialized in traditional Moroccan carpets. The intricate patterns and colors of the carpets drew him in, and he was introduced to Karim, a master weaver with decades of experience.

Karim's workshop was a hive of activity, with looms clacking rhythmically and artisans working meticulously on their creations. Mark was fascinated by the intricate process of carpet weaving, which combined artistry, patience, and an intimate knowledge of traditional techniques. Karim took the time to explain the significance of different patterns and colors, each telling a unique story of the region's history and culture.

Mark spent two afternoons in the workshop, learning the basics of weaving and helping with small tasks. This hands-on experience made him appreciate the skill and dedication required to create these beautiful pieces of art. He also learned about the economic challenges faced by artisans like Karim, who struggled to maintain their craft in the face of modern pressures and competition from mass-produced goods.

During his time in Marrakech, Mark also became involved with a local non-profit organization focused on education and empowerment for young girls. The organization aimed to provide opportunities for girls from disadvantaged backgrounds to access quality education and vocational training. Mark volunteered to teach English for 2 days and assist with various activities, forming strong bonds with the students for these days.

One of the girls, named Leila, stood out to Mark for her intelligence and determination. Despite facing significant obstacles, Leila was determined to become a teacher and inspire other girls in her community. Her story moved Mark deeply.

Together, Mark and the organization arranged a one day workshop that included language lessons, computer skills, and art projects. These workshops not only provided practical skills but also built the girls' confidence and fostered a sense of community and support. Mark was inspired by their enthusiasm and dedication, and he found immense fulfillment in contributing to their growth and development.

In Djemaa El Fna, he immersed himself in their spiritual practices, attending yoga retreats and meditation sessions. The serene beaches, lush rice terraces, and the gentle rhythm of the city center provided a perfect setting for introspection. He learned about the importance of mindfulness, of being present in the moment and appreciating the simple joys of life.

One particular experience in Djemaa El Fna stood out. This was a visit to a traditional healer, a wise old woman known for her deep spiritual insights. She performed a cleansing ritual, using herbs and chants to release negative energy and restore balance.

The ritual was a deeply emotional experience for Mark. It was as if the weight of his grief and guilt had been lifted, leaving him with a sense of lightness.

In the evenings, Mark often found himself drawn to the Djemaa el-Fna square, the heart of Marrakech. Here, he encountered a wide array of performers, from snake charmers and acrobats to musicians and storytellers. One storyteller, in particular, caught his attention. An elderly man named Mohammad captivated large crowds with his mesmerizing tales of adventure, love, and wisdom.

Intrigued by Mohammad's skill, Mark approached him after one performance and struck up a conversation. Mohammad welcomed him warmly and shared the history of his craft, emphasizing the role of storytelling in preserving cultural heritage and imparting moral lessons. Mark was fascinated by Mohammad's ability to weave complex narratives that went well with people of all ages and backgrounds.

Mohammad invited Mark to join him in one of his storytelling sessions, encouraging him to share his own experiences and observations from his travels. Though initially hesitant, Mark found the courage to speak, drawing upon his encounters and the lessons he had learned along the way. The audience's positive reaction bolstered his confidence and reinforced his belief in the power of storytelling as a means of connection and understanding.

In the evenings, as the call to prayer echoed across the city, Mark often found himself drawn to the community gatherings that unfolded in Marrakech's public squares. One particular evening, he joined a group of young locals participating in a spirited discussion about their aspirations and the challenges they faced in a rapidly changing world. They spoke of dreams constrained by economic realities and societal expectations, yet there was a palpable sense of hope and determination in their voices.

Among them was Latifa, a young woman pursuing a degree in environmental science, driven by a desire to address the pressing issue of water scarcity in her region. Her passion for sustainability and her innovative ideas for water conservation left a deep impression on Mark. Through her, he saw how vulnerability, acknowledging the fragility of their environment, could be a powerful motivator for change and progress.

Latifa grew up in a small village where water was a precious commodity. Every drop mattered, and the community had developed intricate methods to ensure that nothing was wasted. She recounted how, as a child, she would accompany her grandmother to the village well, where they would collect water in clay pots. The journey was long, and the pots were heavy, but it was a daily reminder of the value of water and the importance of conservation.

Inspired by these early experiences, Latifa pursued her education with a relentless determination. She spoke to Mark about her latest project which was centered around a rainwater harvesting system designed to provide clean water to her village. The system was simple yet ingenious, using rooftops to collect rainwater, which was then filtered and stored in large underground tanks. This provided a reliable source of water during the dry season and also reduced the community's dependence on distant wells.

Mark was captivated by Latifa's dedication and the tangible impact of her work. She explained how the project had not only alleviated water scarcity but had also brought people together within the village. Everyone contributed, from the elders who shared traditional knowledge about water conservation to the children who helped with the construction and maintenance of the system.

As they walked through the village, Latifa pointed out the flourishing gardens and lush greenery that had sprung up since the implementation of the rainwater harvesting system. The transformation was remarkable. Areas that were once barren and dry were now blossoming with life, all thanks to the power of collective action and sustainable practices.

Latifa also shared her plans for the future. She was working on a larger initiative to introduce solar-powered water pumps, which would further enhance the community's access to clean water. She envisioned a future where her village, and others like it, could thrive despite the challenges posed by climate change and environmental degradation.

Mark found Latifa's story deeply inspiring. It taught him that even in the face of daunting challenges, individuals could make a significant difference. Latifa's work was a beacon of hope, showing that with passion, innovation, and community support, sustainable solutions were within reach.

Through his conversations with Latifa, Mark realized the importance of vulnerability in driving change. Acknowledging the fragility of their environment had empowered Latifa and her community to take proactive steps toward sustainability. This lesson reinforced his belief in the power of individual and collective action.

As Mark continued his journey, he carried Latifa's story with him, sharing it with others and drawing inspiration from her unwavering commitment to creating a better world. Latifa's story was a pivotal chapter in Mark's journey, a reminder that the path to healing and growth often involved looking beyond oneself and finding ways to contribute to the greater good. Latifa's story, and others like it, serve as a reminder that even the smallest actions can have a large impact, and that together, they can create a world where everyone has the opportunity to thrive.

Mark also spent time with local musicians who gathered in Jemaa el-Fna square. These artists, who played traditional Moroccan instruments and shared their culture through music, taught Mark about the healing power of artistic expression. One musician, Omar, recounted his personal struggles with health issues and how music had been his solace and strength. Mark realized that, much like Omar, he could channel his emotions and experiences into creative outlets, finding a way to express and process his grief.

In the quieter moments, Mark visited the tranquil gardens of Marrakech, like Jardin Majorelle. Here, surrounded by exotic plants and vibrant colors, he found a sanctuary for reflection. The peaceful ambiance allowed him to meditate on his journey and the lessons he had learned from those he met. Each encounter and story added a layer of depth to his understanding of resilience and vulnerability.

Fatima invited Mark to join her family for a traditional Moroccan meal one evening. As they sat around a low table, sharing tagine and freshly baked bread, Mark observed the strong familial bonds and the mutual support that defined their lives. The sense of belonging was a stark contrast to the isolation he had felt after his father's passing. Through this experience, he realized that strength often comes from leaning on others and allowing oneself to be supported.

During his time in Marrakech, Mark also encountered activists working on social justice issues. He met with a group focused on empowering women and girls through education and vocational training. The stories of women who had triumphed over substantial challenges to fulfill their dream were deeply moving and motivational. These experiences strengthened Mark's understanding of how people unite to support each other, showcasing their shared strength during challenging times.

Mark's time in Marrakech culminated in a memorable community event organized by the non-profit. The event showcased the talents and achievements of the girls he had worked with, as well as the artisans and performers he had met. It was a joyful acknowledgment of the strength to overcome, creativity, and the diverse cultural heritage of Marrakech.

As the event came to a close, Mark was filled with gratitude. He was happy that he contributed to the community and that he has also grown personally through his interactions and experiences. The fortitude and strength he had witnessed in the people of Marrakech had left an indelible mark on him, shaping his perspective and deepening his understanding of what it meant to overcome adversity and find strength in vulnerability.

Mark felt a mix of emotions as he departed from Marrakech. The city had become a second home, a place where he had forged meaningful connections and learned invaluable lessons. As he boarded the plane, he looked back at the city one last time, carrying with him the stories, lessons, and spirit of Marrakech, ready to face whatever lay ahead on his trip.

Chapter 5: Rediscovering Family Bonds

As Mark Reynolds continued his journey, he felt an increasing pull towards home. The roads he traveled and the people he met had taught him priceless lessons. But there was an unfinished chapter in his story that awaited him back where it all began, and that was his family. The call to reconnect with loved ones grew louder, urging him to explore the ties that had always been there but were often taken for granted. It was time to rediscover the bonds that defined his sense of belonging and identity.

Reconnecting with Loved Ones

Returning to his hometown was a bittersweet experience. The familiar streets, the scent of blossoming flowers, and the old brick houses all brought back memories. Yet, there was also a palpable sense of apprehension. Mark had left with unresolved emotions and unspoken words that now demanded his attention. The journey had changed him, and he hoped that these changes would pave the way for healing and deeper connections.

One of his first visits was to his mother, Susan. Time had etched its marks on her face, but her eyes still sparkled with the warmth and love he remembered. Their relationship had been strained after his father's passing, the weight of grief creating a chasm between them. Over cups of herbal tea in the sunlit kitchen where he had spent countless mornings as a child, they began to talk, really talk, for the first time in years.

Susan shared stories of her own struggles, the silent battles she had fought to keep the family together. Her openness revealed a strength Mark had never fully appreciated. They laughed, they cried, and through these moments, the distance that had grown between them began to shrink. Susan's stories about his father, anecdotes filled with love and wisdom, became bridges connecting past to present, allowing Mark to see his father through her eyes as a husband, a friend, and a partner.

As they spent more time together, Mark noticed how much he had missed the simple, everyday moments with his mother, the shared meals, the walks in the garden, and the comforting routine of family life. He began to grasp the depth of his mother's inner strength, realizing that her fortitude had not only kept the family going but also provided a solid ground for him to rebuild his own sense of identity.

Mark's return also brought about a reconnection with old friends. One such friend was David, his best friend from high school, who immediately came when he heard of Mark's return . They had shared countless memories, from mischievous escapades to deep, philosophical discussions about life. David had always been a steadfast presence in Mark's life, and their friendship had ensured many challenges.

Meeting David after a long time was more like stepping back in time. They talked about their respective journeys, the ups and downs, and the lessons learned. David, now a successful author, shared his own experiences of loss and healing. David's unwavering support and understanding provided Mark with the reassurance that true friendships could endure time and distance.

As Mark re-established these connections, he realized that his journey had come full circle. The experiences and lessons from his travels had equipped him with a newfound appreciation for the relationships that had shaped him. He understood that healing was not just an individual process but one that was enriched by the support and love of those around him.

The process of reconnecting with loved ones also helped Mark confront the emotions he had long suppressed. The memories of his father, which once brought only pain, now brought a sense of warmth and comfort. Through the stories shared by his mother, he began to see his father's influence in all aspects of his life, in his values, and his capacity for love.

Healing Together

Mark and his mum reached out to his siblings, each scattered in different cities, living lives molded by their unique experiences and the common thread of their shared history. His sister, Emily, and brother, John, had been his closest allies growing up, but over the years, their lives had taken different paths. Emily, a dedicated teacher, and John, a busy architect, had their own families and responsibilities. Emily had always been the mediator, the one who tried to keep everyone together. Mark remembered the countless times she had tried to bridge the gaps during family gatherings.

Reconnecting with them meant finding time amidst their hectic schedules, but it was a priority Mark was determined to make.

One weekend, they planned a family picnic at the park where they had played as children. The day was filled with laughter and nostalgia as they reminisced about their shared childhood adventures. Watching his nephews play together, Mark felt truly happy. These moments of connection were more than just reliving the past; they were about building a future where family ties were strong and supportive.

Emily and John shared their own experiences of dealing with their father's loss. Emily spoke about how she had channeled her grief into her work, finding comfort in teaching and mentoring young minds. John revealed that he had often found himself visiting the places their father had loved, drawing inspiration from the memories to fuel his creative projects. These conversations were cathartic, helping Mark understand that he was not alone in his grief and that each of them had found unique ways to cope and honor their father's legacy.

The siblings visited a quaint lakeside cabin where they had spent many summer vacations. The air was filled with the scent of pine and the sound of water lapping against the shore, a perfect setting for rekindling their bond. They cooked meals together, reminiscing about their childhood adventures and mischief. They took long walks, sharing their lives, their fears, and their hopes.

Emily spoke about the pressure she felt to be the glue that held everyone together, a role she had accepted willingly but which had taken its toll. Mark's younger brother, James, opened up about his struggles with feeling overshadowed by the memories of their father and the expectations placed upon him. Through these conversations, they discovered that each of them had been carrying their own burdens, shaped by the same loss but processed differently.

The act of sharing their individual grief and struggles became a collective healing process. They acknowledged their pain and allowed themselves to be vulnerable, creating a space where empathy and understanding could flourish. The siblings realized that their father's legacy wasn't just about living up to his achievements but about supporting one another, just as he had always tried to do.

Sharing Stories of Dad

One of the most meaningful moments came when they decided to honor their father's memory by sharing stories about him. Each story, whether joyful, poignant, or humorous, painted a multifaceted picture of a man who had deeply impacted their lives. Emily recalled the time their father had spent an entire weekend helping her build a science project, turning it into a memorable bonding experience. James shared a story about their father's unwavering support during a particularly tough year in school, emphasizing his role as a mentor and guide.

Mark, too, had his stories, memories of fishing trips, late-night talks, and the quiet wisdom imparted during everyday moments. He realized that these stories were more than just recollections; they were lessons in strength, love, and the importance of family. Each anecdote became a thread in the texture of their father's legacy, intertwining together the values and principles he had instilled in them.

As they shared these stories, the siblings found themselves laughing and crying, their emotions ebbing and flowing like the tides. It was an experience, one that allowed them to celebrate their father's life while acknowledging the void his absence had left. They understood that while the pain of loss would never fully disappear, it could coexist with the joy of remembering and honoring the man who had shaped their lives.

Mark's favorite story to share was about a particular fishing trip they had taken to a secluded lake. His father had taught him the patience needed for fishing, but it was more than just the catch that mattered. It was during these quiet moments by the water that his father shared stories of his own youth, lessons learned, and the importance of persistence. Mark remembered the way his father's eyes lit up as he talked about his dreams and aspirations, and how those conversations had instilled a clear direction in him.

Emily's story highlighted their father's playful side. She recalled a rainy day when he had turned their living room into a makeshift camping site, complete with a tent made from blankets and a "campfire" of flashlights and tissue paper. They had roasted marshmallows in the fireplace and told ghost stories late into the night. That memory was a reminder of their father's ability to create magic out of mundane moments, teaching them to find joy and wonder in everyday life.

James brought up a story from their father's career as a teacher. He shared how their father had gone the extra mile to help a struggling student, spending hours after school tutoring and mentoring. The student had eventually turned their academic performance around, and proved their father's dedication and belief in the potential of every individual. This story underscored the impact their father had not only on their lives but on many others as well.

Their mother, Susan, added her own cherished memories, providing a perspective that deepened their understanding of their father as more than a companion. She spoke of the early days of their marriage, the dreams they had shared, and the challenges they had overcome together. Her stories revealed a side of their father that was nurturing and supportive, highlighting the quiet strength of their bond.

She began by talking about the early days of their marriage, painting a picture of two young lovers with big dreams and even bigger hearts. She described their first tiny apartment, which had been modest and humble but filled with love and laughter.

Despite the financial struggles, they had built a life together brick by brick, supporting each other through thick and thin. She reminisced about their spontaneous road trips, where they would pack up the car and drive with no particular destination in mind. These adventures, though simple, were some of the most cherished memories of their life together. One particular trip to the mountains stood out. They had gotten lost on a winding road but ended up discovering a secluded spot by a river, where they spent the day swimming and talking about their aspirations for the future. Truly their father had an adventurous spirit and has the ability to turn unexpected situations into treasured moments.

Susan also spoke of the tough times, sharing how they had navigated the challenges of parenthood and the pressures of their careers. She recounted the sleepless nights when their children were infants, the stressful act of balancing work and family, and the emotional toll of supporting each other through personal losses and setbacks. Her voice softened as she talked about the miscarriage they had suffered between Emily and James. It had been a heart-wrenching experience, but it had also brought them closer together, strengthening their bond and deepening their empathy for each other.

She talked about the quieter moments too, especially the Sunday afternoons spent gardening, the evenings spent reading by the fire, and the unspoken understanding that developed between them over the years. These stories revealed a side of their father who always found joy in the simple pleasures of life and who was always there to lend a helping hand or a listening ear.

One particularly touching story was about the time when Susan had fallen seriously ill. Their father had taken on the role of caregiver, managing the household, looking after the children, and nursing her back to health. His unwavering support during those trying times exemplified the depth of his love and commitment. Susan's eyes filled with tears as she spoke about the gratitude she felt for having such a devoted partner. As Susan shared these stories, the siblings were struck by the depth of their parents' relationship and the strength of their father's character. They began to see their father as a parent and also as a man who had lived a full and rich life, marked by both triumphs and trials. Susan's insights provided a more complete picture of the man they had loved and admired, helping them to understand and appreciate the legacy he had left behind.

Together, these stories painted a rich picture of their father, transforming their grief into a celebration of his life. They realized that their father's essence lived on in their collective memories and the values he had shared. This storytelling session became a decisive moment in their journey of healing, allowing them to reconnect with each other and with the memory of their father in a meaningful way.

Mark found that these shared stories honored his father's memory and also reinforced the importance of family bonds. And even though their father was no longer physically present, his spirit and teachings continued to guide them. This realization brought a sense of peace and acceptance, helping Mark to further embrace his journey of personal transformation and recovery

Embracing Family Traditions

Mark's journey of rediscovery also involved embracing family traditions that had faded over the years. He found comfort in reviving these rituals. One such tradition was the annual family barbecue, a day-long celebration filled with laughter, music, and the delicious aroma of grilled food.

This year, Mark took it upon himself to organize the event, inviting extended family members and close friends. As they gathered in the backyard, the atmosphere was filled with warmth. Children played games on the lawn, while adults shared stories and caught up on each other's lives. The barbecue became a tribute to their father who deeply cherished family, togetherness, and love.

In the weeks leading up to the barbecue, Mark immersed himself in the preparations. He meticulously planned the menu, drawing inspiration from recipes his father had loved. He spent hours in the kitchen with his mother, Susan, recreating family favorites, such as succulent ribs marinated in a secret blend of spices, herbed chicken skewers, and homemade coleslaw with just the right amount of tang. Susan's guidance and stories about past barbecues added an extra layer of meaning to the process, turning it into a bonding experience in itself.

Mark also reached out to his siblings, Emily and James, asking for their input and assistance. Emily, a talented baker, offered to make their father's favorite apple pie, while James, who is particularly skilled in organization, took charge of setting up the backyard and arranging activities for the kids. The planning and collaboration brought them closer, unity that had sometimes been overshadowed by the daily demands of life.

The day of the barbecue arrived with clear skies and a gentle breeze, perfect weather for an outdoor gathering. The backyard was transformed into a lively and welcoming space, with strings of colorful lanterns, picnic tables draped in cheerful clothes, and a cozy seating area around a fire pit for later in the evening. A playlist of their father's favorite tunes played softly in the background, setting a nostalgic yet joyful tone.

As guests began to arrive, Mark felt a mix of excitement and nervousness. He greeted each family member and friend with a warm smile, feeling the genuine affection and support in their hugs and handshakes. The turnout was heartwarming. Cousins, aunts, uncles, old family friends, and even neighbors who had known their father for years came to grace the occasion.

The grilling station became the heart of the gathering, with the enticing aroma of sizzling meat and vegetables wafting through the air. Mark manned the grill with the same enthusiasm and care his father had once shown. As he turned the skewers and flipped the burgers, he remembered his father's tips on achieving the perfect char and how those moments at the grill had always been about more than cooking, but also about sharing.

Children ran around playing tag and tossing frisbees. Their laughter became a joyous backdrop to the adult conversations. Emily's apple pie, with its golden crust and sweet filling, was a hit, and she beamed with pride as everyone complimented her baking skills. James organized a few friendly games of horseshoes and corn hole, drawing in participants of all ages and adding to the spirit of fun and togetherness.

Throughout the day, stories flowed as freely as the lemonade and iced tea. Family members reminisced about past barbecues, sharing stories that highlighted their father's humor, generosity, and his love for bringing people together. Mark listened, sometimes chiming in with his own memories, but mostly soaking in the love and admiration that filled each tale. These stories were a collective tribute, a way for everyone to keep his father's spirit alive.

As the sun set, Mark gathered everyone around the fire pit for a special tribute. With a gentle crackle of the fire providing a comforting soundtrack, he thanked everyone for coming and spoke from the heart about what the day meant to him and his family. He talked about his father's legacy, how he valued family, and the love he had instilled in them, and how important it was to continue these traditions.

He then invited everyone to share their favorite memories of his father. The stories ranged from funny and light-hearted to deeply moving, each one adding a piece to the mosaic of his father's life. One of the neighbors recounted how Mark's father had helped him rebuild his porch after a storm, refusing any payment and saying that neighbors should look out for each other. An aunt shared a touching story about a road trip they had taken, during which his father had shown patience and kindness despite the challenges they faced.

As the stories were shared, Mark felt so happy. He began to trust so much in the enduring power of family bonds, that even in the face of loss, these connections could be nurtured and strengthened. The barbecue was a symbol of collective strength, a way to honor the past while building a foundation for the future.

After the last story was told and the fire had burned down to glowing embers, Mark took a moment to reflect on the day. He looked around at the faces of his loved ones, illuminated by the soft light of the lanterns and the fire. There was a palpable sense of peace and contentment, a feeling that despite the pain of their father's absence, they had found a way to celebrate his life and keep his memory alive.

Mark realized that the barbecue honored his father, but more importantly, rekindled the family's sense of unity and purpose. The shared stories and laughter had woven new threads of connection, strengthening their bonds and creating new memories to cherish. He felt grateful for the journey that had brought him back home, for the lessons learned along the way, and for the opportunity to reconnect with his roots.

As he hugged his mother goodnight and walked her to the door, Susan squeezed his hand and said, "Your father would have been so proud of you today." Those words made Mark feel accomplished and gave him inner peace. He knew that as he was healing, he had, in this process, taken a significant step forward, one filled with love, remembrance, and the promise of new beginnings.

A Deeper Understanding of Legacy

Through these experiences, Mark gained a deeper understanding of what it meant to carry on his father's legacy. It wasn't about living in his shadow or replicating his achievements but about embodying the values he had imparted, such as integrity, kindness, and the importance of family.

Mark's journey had taken him across continents, but it was in the rediscovery of family bonds that he found the most meaningful revelations. The strength he had witnessed in Tokyo, and Marrakech were mirrored in the faces of his loved ones. Their shared history, their collective struggles, and their unwavering support became the bedrock upon which Mark could build his future.

Chapter 6: Embracing Self-Discovery

Mark Reynolds' journey of self-exploration was not a single, defining moment but a gradual unfolding, an awakening that took him to places both external and internal. The paths he walked were as varied as the landscapes he encountered. Each step led him closer to understanding himself. The quest to find himself again, was a mosaic of experiences, reflections, and revelations that reshaped his identity and purpose.

Embracing a New Identity

Through these diverse experiences, Mark began to embrace a new identity, one that was not defined by his past or the expectations of others but by his own values and aspirations. He got to know that self-discovery was not about becoming someone else but about uncovering the true self that had always been there, hidden beneath layers of fear and doubt.

In each city he visited, Mark found pieces of himself that he had forgotten or never known existed. He learned to embrace his vulnerabilities, to acknowledge his strengths, and to accept his imperfections. It was a continuous process, a lifelong endeavor that required patience, courage, and an open heart.

As he returned home, he felt a sense of completion, a feeling that he had found what he was looking for. The journey had equipped him with the understanding and determination he needed to move forward confidently and with a clear direction. He knew that the road ahead would still have its challenges, but he felt better equipped to face them, armed with the lessons he had learned and the self-awareness he had gained.

As he reconnected with his family and friends, sharing his experiences and the wisdom he had acquired, he found joy in the simple moments. He found out that spending time with loved ones, pursuing his passions, and living a life that was true to himself, brought him more joy than anything else. The journey did not transform him into a different person. Rather it changed him into a more authentic version of himself.

Finding closure and moving forward

One of the habits Mark formed was revisiting places that held special memories of his father. On a certain day, He traveled to their old family cabin in the Blue Ridge Mountains, a place where they had spent countless weekends fishing, hiking, and sharing stories around the campfire. As he walked through the trails and sat by the serene lake, Mark felt his father's presence strongly. The memories were vivid and comforting to him.

At the cabin, Mark found his father's journal, tucked away in a drawer. Reading through the entries, he discovered thoughts and reflections that his father had never shared with anyone. The journal was a treasure trove of wisdom, humor, and love. It was a perfect reminder of the man his father had always been highlighting his struggles, his triumphs, and his dreams. Through his father's words, Mark felt a renewed connection and a sense of closure. His father's legacy was not just in the memories they had made but also in the lessons he had imparted and the values he had instilled in them.

Mark continues to honor his father's legacy by organizing community events in his memory. Each time, he invites family, friends, and neighbors to celebrate his father's life, sharing stories and memories that showcase his father's profound impact. These gatherings are filled with laughter, tears, and a deep sense of connection, offering meaningful experiences for Mark and others as they reflect on how his father's kindness and generosity continue to touch many lives. These events affirm that his father's spirit will endure through the lasting influence he had on others.

Resolving Unanswered Questions

As part of his journey towards closure, Mark also sought to resolve the unanswered questions that had lingered since his father's passing. He reached out to his father's old colleagues and friends, seeking to understand the aspects of his father's life that he had not known. These conversations revealed facets of his father's personality and experiences that were previously hidden from Mark. He learned about his father's struggles at work, his aspirations, and the challenges he had faced at work.

One particularly enlightening conversation was with his father's best friend, George, who shared stories of their youth and adventures together. George spoke of his father's ambitions, the obstacles he had overcome, and the principles he had lived by. These stories filled in the gaps of Mark's understanding, painting a fuller picture of his father's life. Through these interactions, Mark gained a deeper appreciation of his father's journey and the sacrifices he had made.

Mark also took the time to revisit the letters and cards his father had written to him over the years. Each piece of correspondence showcased his father's love and care. Mark found comfort and understanding in the words, providing him with reassurance and perspective. He found comfort in knowing that his father had always been proud of him, even during times when Mark had doubted himself. These letters were a source of strength, helping Mark to let go of any lingering regrets and to move forward with a clear heart.

Embracing Life Anew

With a sense of closure, Mark began to embrace his future with renewed optimism. He realized that moving forward wasn't just about forgetting his father but carrying his memory in a way that uplifted and motivated him. Mark started to set new goals and aspirations, driven by the lessons he had learned from his journey. He returned to his passion for writing, using his experiences as a foundation for his stories.

Mark also reconnected with his community, volunteering at local shelters and participating in neighborhood projects. He found joy in giving back, realizing that his father's legacy of kindness could be perpetuated through his own actions. The act of helping others provided a sense of purpose and fulfillment, reinforcing the values his father had taught him.

Strengthening Family Bonds

He strengthened his relationships with his family. He spent more time with his mother, sharing memories of his father and supporting each other through their grief. They began to create new traditions, honoring his father's memory while building their own future. Mark also reached out to his siblings, mending old rifts and fostering a renewed sense of unity. Together, they created a family scrapbook, filled with photos, letters, and stories that celebrated their father's life.

Spending time with his mother, Susan, became a cornerstone of Mark's adventure. They would sit for hours in the sunlit kitchen, the same room where his father's laughter once filled the air. Over cups of herbal tea, they would share memories of his father, recollections that were joyful and sweet. Susan would speak of the early days of their marriage, painting a picture of a man who was unique in his own ways, a man who was always there for her no matter the circumstance. Mark would listen intently, each story deepening his understanding and appreciation of his father.

One evening, Susan brought out an old photo album. It was filled with pictures from family vacations, birthday parties, and everyday moments that captured the essence of their family life. They laughed at the old hairstyles and fashion choices, but also found joy in these visual memories. Each photograph captured the love and bond they shared, reminding them that while his father was gone, his spirit remained a part of their lives.

Determined to keep his father's memory alive while building a future for themselves, Mark and his mother started creating new traditions. One of these was a weekly family dinner, where they would cook his father's favorite dishes and invite relatives and friends to join them. The dinners became a space for storytelling, where everyone felt free to share their thoughts and emotions. These gatherings honored their father's memory but at the same time, it strengthened the family's bonds, creating a sense of continuity and belonging.

Another tradition they started was an annual visit to his father's favorite fishing spot. Mark, his mother, and siblings would spend the day fishing, just as they had done with his father. It was a way to reconnect with nature, reflect on their memories, and feel close to him in a place he loved. These trips became a cherished time for the family, blending remembrance with the creation of new, joyful experiences.

Every year, as the family packed up their fishing gear and set off for the serene lake nestled in the woods, there was an air of anticipation and excitement. The journey itself became part of the tradition. They would take the same winding road, passing landmarks that sparked conversations about past trips and their father's love for this tranquil escape. The old oak tree by the side of the road, the charming farmhouse with its colorful flower garden, and the bridge that creaked under their car's weight all became markers of their pilgrimage.

Upon arriving at the lake, the family would set up their base camp with blankets, picnic baskets, and folding chairs. The crystal clear water mirrored the sky, and the gentle rustling of leaves provided a soothing soundtrack. Mark's mother, Susan, always brought along his father's old fishing hat, placing it on a rock near the water's edge as a silent tribute. It was a small gesture, but it held deep meaning, symbolizing his enduring presence.

As they cast their lines into the water, the family engaged in light-hearted banter and shared stories. Each cast was accompanied by laughter and the occasional friendly competition about who would catch the first fish. Mark often found himself reminiscing about his father's patient teaching, recalling the way his father's hands had guided his on the fishing rod, and the proud smile when he caught his first fish.

The fishing trips created new memories and strengthened their family bond. One year, Mark's sister Emily caught a particularly large fish. The excitement was palpable as they all gathered around to marvel at her catch. They took photos, their smiles wide and genuine, knowing that this moment would be added to their scrapbook of cherished memories.

As the day progressed, there were quieter moments of reflection. The family would find their own spots along the shore, gazing out over the shimmering water. Mark often sat on a weathered log, the same spot where his father used to sit, and let his thoughts wander. It was during these moments that he felt his father's presence the most, a comforting sense of connection with his father.

Susan would sometimes paint vivid pictures of their youthful adventures and dreams. These stories added layers to Mark's understanding of his parents, deepening his appreciation for the life they had built together. His mother's voice, filled with both sorrow and joy, painted a picture of memories that embraced them all.

As the sun began to set, the family would gather around a campfire. The crackling flames mirrored the warmth in their hearts as they roasted marshmallows and shared their hopes and dreams. The firelight danced on their faces, illuminating the love and strength that bound them together.

Mark often took this time to reflect on the lessons his father had imparted. He would share these with his siblings, turning the fishing trips into opportunities for mutual support in the family. Reflecting on how their father had faced challenges with unwavering determination gives them a positive outlook. These discussions became a source of encouragement, helping them navigate their own paths with courage and grace.

The annual fishing trip became a tradition and a celebration of life. Each year, as they packed up to leave, they felt a renewed sense of closeness and purpose.

Building New Traditions

The tradition also evolved over time. Mark's nephews and nieces, who had never met their grandfather, joined the trips, adding a new dimension to the experience. The children's curiosity and enthusiasm breathed new life into the tradition, as they eagerly learned to fish and listened wide-eyed to stories about their grandfather. These trips became a bridge between generations, passing down values and memories that shaped the family's identity.

One particularly memorable year, Mark organized a small fishing tournament for the family. Everyone participated, from the youngest to the oldest, and the lake echoed with laughter and cheers. The tournament ended with a simple prize, a handcrafted trophy that Mark had made which symbolized the family's unity and fortitude. The winner, Mark's youngest nephew, proudly held the trophy high, a lovely sight for everyone to behold.

A Lasting Legacy

As the family grew and changed, the annual fishing trip remained a constant part of their life. It became a beacon of continuity amidst life's ups and downs. It was a time to honor the past, embrace the present while still looking forward to the future with hope and determination. The fishing spot, once just a place of recreation, had become a sacred ground where memories were cherished, and new ones were created.

Each year, as they returned to the lake, they reaffirmed their bonds, carrying forward the tradition of a father who had taught them the true meaning of family.

Mark also made a concerted effort to reach out to his siblings regularly, Emily and James. Over the years, life's demands and the weight of grief had created distance between them. Mark knew that to truly honor their father's memory, it was essential to mend these old rifts and foster a renewed sense of unity.

He began by inviting Emily and James to join him and their mother for weekly dinners. At first, the conversations were tentative, filled with polite small talk and careful steps around deeper issues. But gradually, the shared meals became a safe space for open dialogue. They reminisced about their childhood adventures, shared their struggles and triumphs, and began to understand each other's perspectives and emotions better.

One of the most meaningful projects they undertook together was creating a family scrapbook. It started as a simple idea which involved compiling photos and letters that celebrated their father's life, but it quickly grew into a labor of love that brought the family even closer. They gathered at Susan's house one weekend, armed with old photo albums, boxes of letters, and cherished mementos.

As they sifted through the piles of memories, they shared interesting stories about their father. Emily found a letter their father had written to her on her first day of college, filled with words of encouragement and pride. James unearthed a series of postcards from their father's business trips, each one detailing his adventures and expressing how much he missed his family. Mark contributed a collection of fishing licenses and lures.

They spent hours arranging the photos and letters in the scrapbook, carefully selecting captions and decorations that reflected their father's personality. The process was both bonding. The scrapbook became a tangible representation of their love, a family treasure that they could pass down to future generations.

Through these efforts, the family rediscovered a sense of unity that had been overshadowed by their bereavement and life's challenges. The weekly dinners, the new traditions, and the collaborative scrapbook project all contributed to rebuilding their relationships and creating a stronger, more cohesive family unit.

Mark found that as they opened up to each other and shared their memories, they also shared their pain and how they have been able to alleviate this. The process of reconnecting and creating new traditions allowed them to support each other in ways they hadn't before. They learned to appreciate the different ways each of them grieved and came out of it, and to respect the unique contributions each person made to the family's journey.

As the months passed, these strengthened relationships became a source of comfort and support for Mark. He realized that while the journey of rediscovery had taken him far from home, the most significant discoveries were made within his own family.
The bonds they rebuilt and the new traditions they created became the cornerstone of their shared recovery and development.

The family scrapbook, now a cherished heirloom, symbolized their resilience and unity. It served as a reminder that their father's legacy lived on through their love and memories. Every time they added a new photo or letter, they honored his memory and celebrated their ongoing journey together.

Mark's efforts to strengthen his family relationships brought him closer to his mother, siblings, and extended family. It also helped him find a deeper sense of peace and fulfillment. He realized that although the pain of loss would always linger, the love and connections they nurtured would flourish, offering strength and comfort for years to come. He found peace in knowing that these relationships would serve as a source of support, helping them navigate future challenges. Truthfully, amidst sorrow, there is always room for growth and joy.

A New Chapter

Mark's journey towards finding closure and moving forward was not just about healing from his father's loss but also about embracing his own life's potential. He enrolled in a creative writing course, where he honed his skills and found a supportive community of fellow writers. The process of writing became a powerful outlet for his emotions, allowing him to express his grief, joy, and everything in between.

He also embarked on new adventures, traveling to places he had always wanted to visit. In the bustling streets of New York City, he found inspiration in the diverse cultures and vibrant energy. He visited the serene landscapes of New Zealand, where the natural beauty and tranquility provided a perfect setting for reflection and renewal.

Each place he visited offered a unique perspective, deepening his understanding of the world and his role in it. With every new destination, he discovered diverse cultures and experiences that broadened his horizons and reshaped his worldview. These odysseys enriched his knowledge and also fostered a greater appreciation for humanity. As he immersed himself in different environments, he found himself reflecting on his own beliefs and values, gaining insights that would guide him in his personal and professional life.

The experiences he gathered along the way were like pieces of a puzzle, gradually coming together to form a complete picture of his life's purpose.

Final Reflections

As Mark reflected on his journey, he understood that finding resolution and progressing was a continuous process. Each step he took brought new challenges and lessons, reminding him that healing wasn't a destination but a lifelong endeavor. He recognized that every moment of reflection, every interaction, and every decision contributed to his growth. Mark saw that embracing this ongoing journey required patience and resilience, allowing himself the grace to evolve at his own pace. Over time, he found solace in the gradual progress, appreciating the small victories and the deepening sense of peace that came with each passing day.

It was about accepting the past, cherishing the memories, and using them as a foundation for the future. The pain of loss would always be a part of him, but it no longer defined him. Instead, it became a source of strength guiding him towards a life of meaning.

By embracing his father's legacy, resolving unanswered questions, and looking towards the future with hope, Mark found a way to respect his history while shaping a more promising future.

Conclusion: The Journey Continues

As Mark Reynolds reflects on his incredible journey, he is filled with a sense of gratitude and peace. What began as an overwhelming call of grief after his father's passing has transformed into a path of reflection, resilience, and self-discovery. His father's death was what set him on this journey, but it was the love, lessons, and memories his father left behind that guided him through each step.

From embracing the raw pain of loss to setting out on a pilgrimage of self-discovery,

Mark learned that true healing comes from facing our deepest fears and embracing the unknown with courage and an open heart. The moments of clarity and insight he experienced often emerged in the most unexpected places, indicating that life's greatest lessons are sometimes hidden in its quietest corners.

Reflecting on the adversity he faced, Mark realizes that resilience is not about being unbreakable but about finding strength in vulnerability. The challenges he encountered were stepping stones that led him to a deeper understanding of himself and the world around him. These experiences taught Mark that growth often comes from the most difficult trials and that within each struggle lies the potential for real transformation.

Rediscovering family bonds was a crucial part of Mark's journey. By reestablishing ties with his loved ones, he discovered comfort and a revitalized sense of unity. Sharing stories, mending old wounds, and creating new memories allowed him to honor his father. This journey brought Mark closer to his family, and he was able to acknowledge that family is not just a source of support but a base upon which we build our lives.

Embracing self-discovery proved to be challenging and at the same time, rewarding for Mark. It required him to confront his fears, accept his flaws, and recognize his strengths. Through this process, he gained new perspectives and uncovered personal truths that had been buried beneath years of expectations and doubts. He learned to turn his pain into a driving force using his experiences to help others who might be on similar paths.

Mark has come to know that progressing forward was not about leaving his father behind but about carrying his memory in a way that enriches his life. His father's memory lives on in the values he instilled, the wisdom he shared, and the love he gave. As Mark steps into the future, he does so with a heart full of gratitude and a spirit ready to embrace whatever comes next.

This journey has taught him that life is a continuous process of learning, growing, and evolving. The road ahead is still filled with unknowns, but he is no longer afraid. He has found his path and he is prepared to face it with bravery, strength, and a deep sense of purpose.

To those reading Mark's story, it is hoped that his journey offers consolation, understanding, and motivation. If you are grappling with loss or searching for meaning, remember that healing is possible and that every step you take brings you closer to a place of peace and understanding. Embrace your journey with an open heart, and trust that the answers you seek will reveal themselves in time.

Mark's path was not an easy one, but it was one that led him to absolute truths about the strength of the human spirit and the importance of connection. His story shows that even in our darkest moments, there is a way forward. Whether it was through the warmth of a mother's embrace, the shared laughter of siblings, or the silent communion with nature, each step Mark took was a step toward healing.

As you navigate your own journey, remember that it's okay to feel lost or overwhelmed. These feelings are part of the human experience, and they often precede the most significant breakthroughs. Allow yourself the grace to grieve, to feel, and to grow. Like Mark, you may find that the process of healing is not about forgetting or moving on but about integrating your experiences and finding new ways to embrace your past while building your future.

Mark's experiences remind us that flexibility is not about being unbreakable, but about being able to pick up the pieces and create something beautiful from them. His father's memory became a source of strength, guiding him through the challenges he faced and the decisions he made. It is a reminder to all of us that our loved ones live on in the lessons they taught us, the love they gave us, and the memories we hold dear.

As this book concludes, Mark carries forward the lessons he has learned, the love he has felt, and the endurance he has cultivated. His father's spirit will always be a guiding light, reminding him to live fully, love deeply, and cherish every moment. The journey continues, and Mark is ready to embrace it with hope, courage, and an unwavering belief in the beauty of life.

May you find strength in your vulnerability, joy in your connections, and peace in your quest. Mark's story is one among many, showing off the power of love, the significance of family, and the enduring human spirit.

As you close this book, take with you the knowledge that you are not alone. There are others who have walked a similar path, faced similar heartaches, and found their way to healing. Your pain, though unique to you, is also part of the shared human experience. Allow this realization to comfort you, knowing that in the vast network of life, there are countless avenues of compassion, understanding, and support that you can lean on.

Healing is possible. It may not come quickly or easily, but it comes with patience, with perseverance, and with the willingness to embrace the journey. Each step you take, no matter how small, brings you closer to the light. Some days, the progress may feel slow, almost imperceptible, but remember that even the tiniest steps forward are steps toward a brighter future. Trust in the process and in yourself.

The journey ahead is yours to shape. It is filled with infinite possibilities. Each day is a new opportunity to create, to love, and to grow. Embrace it with an open heart, ready to receive the gifts that life has to offer. Be courageous in your pursuit of happiness, unafraid to face the challenges that come your way. Know that within you lies an immense reservoir of strength, one that can carry you through the darkest of times and into the dawn of new beginnings.

In your connections, find joy. Reach out to those who matter to you, and let them know how much they mean. Build bridges, mend broken relationships, and cherish the moments of togetherness. These relationships are the rudiments that intertwine to shape the richness of your life, bringing color, warmth, and meaning to your existence.

As you navigate your journey, allow yourself to be vulnerable. It is in our vulnerability that we find our true strength. By opening your heart, you invite in love, understanding, and the possibility of meaningful relationships.

Do not shy away from your emotions; embrace them, for they are a reflection of your humanity.

And finally, seek peace. Find it in the quiet moments of reflection, in the beauty of nature, in the laughter of loved ones, and in the simple joys of daily life. Peace is not the absence of challenges, but the presence of a strong spirit that can face them with grace and courage.

Mark's story is a reminder of the enduring human spirit and the incredible power of love and family. Let it inspire you to live fully, love deeply, and cherish every moment. The journey is yours, and it is filled with endless possibilities. Embrace it with an open heart and a courageous spirit, knowing that you are capable of incredible deeds.

Epilogue

Reflecting on his father's legacy, Mark has come to understand that the greatest gift his father gave him was the courage to seek his own path. Tim Reynolds was a man of integrity, kindness, and unyielding love, and these qualities have become the cornerstones of Mark's own life. By living in a way that honors his father's memory, Mark has found a sense of purpose and fulfillment that surpasses the pain of loss. As Mark looks to the future, he does so with a heart full of hope and a spirit ready to embrace whatever comes next. The journey of healing and self-discovery is ongoing, and he is committed to walking it with the same courage and resilience that have brought him this far. The road ahead is still filled with unknowns, but Mark faces it with the confidence that he is not alone. He carries with him the love of his family, the lessons of his past, and the unshakeable belief that every step taken brings him closer to a life of meaning and joy. To those who have walked this path with him, whether in person or through the pages of this book, Mark offers his deepest gratitude. Your support, understanding, and shared experiences have been a source of strength. As you continue on your own journeys, may you find the same resilience, wisdom, and peace that Mark has discovered. The journey continues, but it does so with a renewed sense of purpose and a heart open to all the possibilities that life has to offer. Mark Reynolds is ready to embrace the future, honoring his father's memory by living fully, loving deeply, and cherishing every moment. The lessons learned, the love felt, and the resilience built are the guiding lights that will lead him forward, into a life rich with meaning and joy.